Managing Organizational and Societal Challenges of AI

Confronting how artificial intelligence (AI), the Internet of Things (IoT) and big data (BD) analytics are changing how we live, this book examines how these technologies can affect society at large and education and internal and external security in particular. *Managing Organizational and Societal Challenges of AI: Insights from Education and Cyber Security* addresses such questions as:

- What threats does AI pose to today's world, its internal security and broadly understood external security?
- Will AI-based education take away people's will to think and create?
- Why does AI inspire awe in some of us and fear in others?

The book answers these questions by analysing how AI, IoT and data analytics are applied in security and education. This analysis begins with a literature survey of how these technologies bring both opportunities and threats that require responsible governance and global cooperation. The book underscores the necessity of resilience, adaptive strategies and innovative technologies to ensure preparedness for both traditional and non-traditional threats. It also emphasises that sustainable global security requires coordinated efforts, effective governance and multilateral cooperation.

The book continues its analysis by examining the practical applications of AI in management, education and security. Featuring case studies, it highlights how AI supports hazard monitoring, emergency response and sustainable mobility, as well as personalising education, enhancing training and automating administrative tasks. Discussing the opportunities and challenges of AI in education, including the risks of over-reliance, reduced critical thinking and ethical concerns related to data privacy, the book concludes that AI not only offers significant benefits for improving efficiency, security and adaptability but also requires responsible regulation, investment and awareness of its limitations to ensure ethical and sustainable implementation.

Managing Organizational and Societal Challenges of AI

Insights from Education and Cyber Security

Iwona Klonowska, Marek Walancik
and Michał Bukowski

Routledge
Taylor & Francis Group
NEW YORK AND LONDON

Cover: Web Large Image (Public)

First published 2026
by Routledge
605 Third Avenue, New York, NY 10158

and by Routledge
4 Park Square, Milton Park, Abingdon, Oxon, OX14 4RN

Routledge is an imprint of the Taylor & Francis Group, an informa business

ISBN: 978-1-041-08123-4 (hbk)
ISBN: 978-1-041-08193-7 (pbk)
ISBN: 978-1-003-64419-4 (ebk)

DOI: 10.1201/9781003644194

Typeset in Times
by Apex CoVantage, LLC

Access the Support Material: www.routledge.com/9781041081234

Contents

About the authors

Prof. Marek Walancik, PhD, is an educator, author and researcher in the field of education, security and interculturalism. He heads the Department of Pedagogy and is the director of the Centre for Research and Education of Uniformed Services at the WSB Academy in Dąbrowa Górnicza. Since 2018, he has been the chair of the Scientific Council for the Scientific Discipline of Pedagogy, and since 2024, he has been the chair of the Education for Safety Section of the Committee on Pedagogical Sciences of the Polish Academy of Sciences. He is the author of numerous monographs and scientific publications (over 150), including key works on education, safety education, threats and social and intercultural issues. In 2017, he was awarded the Knight's Cross of the Order of Polonia Restituta for his scientific and social achievements. He actively promotes education and activities for safety in the media and social environment. He is a member of many scientific bodies and teams.

Prof. Iwona Klonowska, PhD, is a retired police brigadier general and from 2020 to 2024 was the rector of the Police Academy in Szczytno, Poland. A long-time police officer and academic teacher, she specialises in psychology, pedagogy, internal security and psychotraumatology. Her scientific interests also include criminology and investigative psychology. For many years, she held managerial positions in police organisational units, as well as in police education institutions, where she actively participated in shaping the education system for uniformed services. She was the creator and co-creator of many police training programmes. During her term as rector, studies in the field of cybercrime for police personnel were established, and cooperation was established with key institutions supporting the training of police officers, such as the UKNF. She focuses on the educational role and effects of AI on humans on their mental state, development opportunities and social threats.

She is a graduate of higher education in psychology and social rehabilitation pedagogy. She completed specialised postgraduate studies in transport psychology (University of Warsaw), organisational unit management (WSPol), counselling and psychological assistance (Jagiellonian University in Krakow), public relations (University of Warsaw) and psychotraumatology (EUST). She is a habilitated doctor of social sciences in the field of pedagogy. Author and editor of more than 160 publications that include monographs, scientific articles and expert studies in the field of security, crime prevention and organisation and management in the police, she is the secretary of the Education for Security Section of the Committee on Pedagogical Sciences of the Polish Academy of Sciences. A member of the Polish Psychological Association, she is a long-time editor-in-chief of the magazine *Policja 997* (Police 997) and the scientific journals *Przegląd Policyjny* (Police Review), *Internal Security* (deputy editor-in-chief) and *Resocjalizacja Polska* (Polish Rehabilitation).

During her service in the police and her academic work, she was involved in research projects and international police cooperation. She has been awarded numerous medals and distinctions by the ministry and the state.

Colonel Michał Bukowski, PhD, is the engineer director of the Criminal Service Institute of the Faculty of Security and Legal Sciences at the Police Academy in Szczytno, is a police officer with many years of experience in preventive and criminal services, as well as in the field of operational analysis, and is a graduate of engineering and master's studies in the field of electronics, telecommunications and communications, followed by doctoral studies completed with a doctoral dissertation in technical informatics.

He specialises in internal security, combating criminal offences, cybercrime and the use of modern technologies, especially AI in operational and investigative work. He is the author and co-author of scientific publications in the field of forensics, criminology of internal security, state security, cybercrime and cybersecurity (CS). As the director of the Institute of Criminal Service at the Police Academy in Szczytno, he co-ordinates the scientific and teaching activities of the unit, supervises research work and implements projects related to the development of modern methods and tools, mainly for the criminal service.

Abbreviations

AI	Artificial intelligence
AR	Augmented reality
BD	Big data
BDA	Big data analysis
CS	Cybersecurity DN deep networks
CV	Computer vision
DT	Decision trees
GZM	Upper Silesian Metropolis
IoT	Internet of Things
JSW	Jastrzębie coal company
KNN	K-nearest neighbours
LR	Linear regression
ML	Machine learning
NLP	Natural language processing
NN	Neural network
QC	Quantum computer
RF	Random forest
RL	Reinforcement learning
SC	Smart cities
SL	Supervised learning
UL	Unsupervised learning
VR	Virtual reality
ZTM	Metropolitan Transportation Authority

Introduction

Believe? But in what? We live in times where we have become hostages to technology!

Robots, AI, etc., will surely become part of our lives sooner or later. Or maybe, they already are? There is probably no country in the world today that has not come into contact with AI. What threats does AI pose to today's world, its internal security and broadly understood external security? Will the use of intelligent algorithms, that is AI, in education guarantee us the security of learning about the future, or will it lead to the domination of human existence by machines? Will AI-based education take away people's will to think and create? Doesn't it already reduce learning to mindless copying of information taken from the web?

Why does AI inspire awe in some of us and fear in others? The authors would like to discuss these and many other questions related to our existence, education and future, as well as the internal and external security of the state, supported by a case study. In our opinion, these are, in today's world, concerns that transcend national borders, divisions and, often, from the perspective of recent years, time. The areas on which the authors have based their conclusions and the preceding discussion are, in their view, fundamental – for what could be more important than security and the accompanying education which allows an increased awareness of the changes taking place and the challenges facing civilisation.

The COVID-19 pandemic has caused many of us to re-evaluate a lot of different values. And these years, starting in 2018, have seen the rise of deep networks (DN), machine learning (ML) and AI. The authors have conducted research on the impact of the pandemic on our lives and want to use the materials collected between 2019 and 2021 to present the potential development of threats and advantages associated with the use of AI, the IoT, big data analysis (BDA) and, of course, CS in the broadest sense.

The main outline of the publication is a three-part but thematically connected analysis of the advantages and threats to internal and external state security and broadly understood education from the use of AI, IoT and BDA. In the first part, the authors will present, based on the latest available publications, a balance of gains and losses that appeared on the horizon at the turn of 2024 and 2025, resulting from four main areas of interest. These areas will be AI, IoT, BDA and CS in two scientific fields: Security and education. In

DOI: 10.1201/9781003644194-1

the second part, using the Delphi method, in-depth interviews and their own participant observation, the authors will analyse surveys distributed via the Internet in Poland and Europe, which will enable them to compare the level of knowledge about AI, IoT and BDA among European populations of different cultures, awareness, religions, ages and genders. Access the Support Material: www.routledge.com/9781041081234. The authors assume that the above parameters will differentiate the approach to AI in the broad sense. The third part is a case study of activities undertaken in the Upper Silesian-Zagłębie Metropolis (GZM), such as occupational safety management by Jastrzębska Spółka Węglowa, taking into account prevention, training and health and safety procedures, as well as challenges related to crisis situations that have occurred in the above-mentioned region over the last 30 years, including the possibility of counteracting them using AI, IoT and BDA.

Future technologies and security

1

In 2024, many different technologies are seen as key to the future of Poland, Europe and the world.

AI (Cao et al. 2023) and ML (Fradkov 2020) are the main technologies of the future. Models such as ChatGPT (Wu et al. 2023), DALL-E (Offert 2023) and similar technologies developed by other companies are used in content creation, work automation and user experience personalisation. In addition, there is BDA, process automation and forecasting and optimisation in sectors such as logistics, medicine and energy.

Quantum computers (QCs) (Hidary & Hidary 2021) are a technology used in cryptography (Naser 2021), molecular simulation (Frenkel & Smit 2023), logistics and optimisation. QC have the potential to revolutionise the solving of problems which are currently unattainable for traditional computers.

Advanced energy technologies: Nuclear fusion (Sánchez 2014), which uses technologies such as tokamaks and stellarators (Xu 2016), is close to breakthroughs that are sure to revolutionise energy. In addition, innovative batteries (Borchers et al. 2021) (e.g. lithium iron phosphate and sodium batteries), which can store large amounts of energy, and supercapacitors (Sharma et al. 2019) are being developed. Improvements in solar panels, wind turbines and fuel cells (He et al. 2023) have revolutionised renewable energy.

The IoT and smart cities (SC) are challenges of today's world developed on the basis of 5G (Gai et al. 2021) and 6G (Jiang & Schotten 2021) technologies, which enable ultra-fast data transmission. These technologies support the development of IoT and SC (Lyu & Hao 2021). They also support real-time environmental monitoring, traffic management and infrastructure management systems.

Augmented reality (AR) and virtual reality (VR) technologies enable the development of the metaverse and applications in education, entertainment, medicine and industrial design. These technologies enable more immersive experiences using technologies such as high-resolution AR glasses.

DOI: 10.1201/9781003644194-2

Biotechnology and medicine of the future include technologies such as CRISPR-Cas9 (Barman et al. 2020), which allows for precise gene modification, 3D printing of tissues and organs (Shapira & Dvir 2021) and the development of drugs or therapies tailored to the individual genome of the patient (Sadee et al. 2023).

Another area is robotics and automation. Robots in industry, agriculture (e.g. autonomous machines (Ali et al. 2023)), healthcare (robotic surgery (Li et al. 2023)) and everyday life (home assistants (Shafiullah et al. 2023)) and the humanoid robots (Tong et al. 2024), which can assist in work and care for the elderly, are the machines of the future that have initiated the development of AI.

Materials of the future: Graphene (Tang et al. 2023) and other 2D materials used in electronics, energy and construction or self-repairing materials (Kim et al. 2024) which we use in construction and mechanical engineering are the future materials of today's construction technologies and design tools.

The mobility technology of the future are primarily autonomous vehicles (Olayode et al. 2023) such as cars, delivery drones and mobile robots. Hyperloops (Grosse-Oetringhaus et al. 2023) and other transport technologies are based on innovative concepts of speed and efficiency.

Another technology is Blockchain and Web3 (FrØland et al. 2023). Web3 comprises decentralised applications, NFTs and digital identity, and Blockchain, for example, in business, is nothing more than supply chain tracking, data security and smart contracts.

The last of the important technologies in 2024 is space exploration. Private space missions (Eriksson & Newlove-Eriksson 2023) by SpaceX and Blue Origin or state projects such as missions to the Moon and Mars, combined with the development of space infrastructure, are building the image of new technologies and are linked to the creation of satellites, space stations and research into the extraction of resources in space (Santomartino et al. 2023).

1.1 INTRODUCTION TO AI, IOT, BIG DATA (BD) AND CYBERSECURITY

AI is a field of science and technology concerned with the creation of systems and algorithms capable of supervised simulation of human intelligence. AI systems are designed to perform tasks which require cognitive processes such as automatic and autonomous learning, natural language understanding, image recognition, data analysis, problem-solving, decision-making, and adaptation to new conditions. AI encompasses a variety of approaches, including ML, NN and DL, which allow computers (digital machines) to independently improve their performance based on acquired or provided experience (Murdick et al. 2020). The goal of AI (Astobiza et al. 2021) is to create systems capable of automating complex tasks which would traditionally require human intelligence. AI is designed to support people in making the right decisions, solving complex problems, analysing vast amounts of data, predicting future events and optimising processes in various fields such as medicine, education, industry, logistics and finance. It also aims to increase the efficiency and precision of activities, minimise errors and relieve humans of routine, time-consuming or dangerous tasks. The ultimate goal of AI is to create intelligent, autonomous systems that can adapt to changing conditions and respond dynamically to new challenges, supporting technological development and improving quality of life. AI ethics is defined as the analysis of norms and values and is crucial for building AI systems which respect human rights, transparency and fairness. Ethical frameworks such as "Human-Centric AI" and ethical declarations (e.g. the Montreal Declaration) should support the design of technologies which focus on people and the environment. The lack of global co-ordination in AI regulation is also an important issue, and international cooperation must be sought to ensure that AI serves sustainable development and is consistent with humanistic values.

AI is divided into narrow (weak) AI (ANI – artificial narrow intelligence), which specialises in a single task (e.g. face recognition or data analysis); general AI (AGI – strong artificial intelligence and artificial general intelligence), which is capable of performing any task requiring intelligence; and superintelligence (ASI – artificial superintelligence), which hypothetically surpasses the capabilities of the human mind in every field.

ANI (Haenlein & Kaplan 2019) are AI systems focused on performing specific tasks. Their origins date back to the 1950s, when Alan Turing proposed the Turing test (French 2000), and in 1956, at a conference in Dartmouth, the term "AI" was officially coined. In the 1960s, expert systems such as ELIZA (Shum et al. 2018) and General Problem Solver (Garvey 2021) were developed, which were the first examples of ANI. Successes such as Deep Blue defeating chess champion Garry Kasparov in 1997 and modern technologies such as image and speech recognition are based on ANI. The development of ANI has accelerated significantly thanks to BDA and DL.

AGI (Haenlein & Kaplan 2019) is a continuation of ANI, an attempt to create AI which matches human intelligence in every aspect. The idea of AGI also dates back to the 1950s, when A. Turing pondered thinking machines. In the 1960s and 1970s, enthusiasm for AGI waned due to technological limitations (AI Winter (Van de Sande et al. 2022)), a period from 1980 to 1983 of reduced funding and interest in AI research. Advances in ML and NN since the 2000s have brought this vision closer, but AGI remains hypothetical, with many technological and philosophical challenges.

ASI (Strelkova 2017) is currently mainly hypothetical. The concept originated alongside the idea of AGI, where ASI refers to AI which surpasses human intelligence in all areas. A. Turing and I.J. Good predicted the possibility of an "intelligence explosion" in the 1950s, where AI could improve itself independently. ASI remains a topic of philosophical, ethical and technological debate, and its potential implications are often discussed in literature and in analyses of the future of AI, for example, by E. Musk and N. Bostrom. It may require strict control, as, if mismanaged, it could pose a threat to humanity.

AI like NN can be trained (learnt) using supervised learning (SL), unsupervised learning (UL) and reinforcement learning (RL). SL (Rani et al. 2023) is one of the basic methods in ML in which a model learns from labelled data, with such labels applied, so that the system can predict outcomes for new data not previously known to it. The key elements of SL are the input data (features), which are represented by a set of features (attributes) that describe a phenomenon such as pixels in an image, words in a sentence or customer demographics. The next element is the output (labels). Each input is assigned a label, which is the correct answer (e.g. "dog" in image classification or a number in price prediction). The next is the dataset, which is divided into a training set (the data on which the model learns), a validation set (the data used to optimise the model and avoid overlearning about the system) and a test set (the data used to evaluate the model's performance). There are two types of problems with SL.

The first is classification, where the model predicts specific category labels known to the model, for example, for image recognition (deciding whether there is a cat or a dog in a picture, and each animal will be classified into a particular model, even though it will be, for example, a parrot), email classification (deciding whether a message is spam or non-spam) and sentiment analysis (deciding whether an item is positive or negative). The second is regression. The model predicts continuous values only. It predicts house prices based on their characteristics, it predicts the temperature on a given day based on the data it has, for example, from previous years, or it estimates the demand for a given product based on its supply over several years. The process of SL consists of several stages. The first stage is data preparation: Collecting and labelling data (e.g. labelling images or defining output values in a set), cleaning the data (e.g. removing gaps or eliminating noise) and dividing the data into sets (training, validation and testing). The next step is to train the model. The algorithm processes the input data, trying to find the patterns specified in the task. It uses a loss function (e.g. the difference between the predicted and true labels) to assess the error each input has. Based on the determined error, the model modifies its parameters to improve the prediction using, for example, the simple gradient method (Martens 2020). The next step is to evaluate the trained model.

After training, the previous stage, the model is tested on test data that was not used during the learning process. The evaluation of the trained model includes metrics such as accuracy (accuracy), precision (precision), sensitivity (recall) or mean square error (MSE), depending on the problem adopted at the beginning. The final stage is optimisation, which is nothing more than tuning the hyperparameters of the model (e.g. the number of layers in the neural network (NN) or the learning rate) and solving problems such as overfitting or underfitting the model. The most popular SL algorithms are linear regression (LR) (Su et al. 2012), simple models for regression and classification; decision trees (DT) (random forest (Hu & Szymczak 2023) – RF) for creating hierarchical decisions from data; support vector machines (Sheykhmousa et al. 2020) (SVM), which are models that separate data using hyperplanes; K-nearest neighbours (Peterson 2009) (KNN), classification/regression based on nearest neighbours and NNs (Motie & Raahemi 2024), which are advanced models capable of recognising complex patterns. As with any method, there are advantages and disadvantages.

The advantages of SL are its effectiveness in solving many practical problems, the ability to use multiple data types (text, images and numbers) and known output results that allow for accurate model quality control. The disadvantages of this method are that it requires a large amount of labelled data, which involves time-consuming manual classification; poorly labelled data leads to incorrectly trained models; and models can be prone to overlearning if the learning data is not sufficiently diverse. Nowadays, models trained in a supervised manner are most often used for predicting sales levels; analysing customer behaviour; recommending products to customers; diagnosing diseases from X-ray images; predicting the effects of treatments, speech and image recognition and machine translation or optimising crop levels from weather data. In summary, SL is very versatile but requires well-labelled data and adequate preparation. It is the basis for many modern applications of AI.

UL (Naeem et al. 2023): UL is a type of ML in which algorithms attempt to extract hidden patterns, structures and relationships in data which have no labels or outcomes assigned.

It works on the basis of similarities and differences between the data, with no clear indication of what the "correct" result looks like. The key feature of UL is the absence of any labels. The input data is unlabelled (unclassified), which means that the algorithm is not given information about the expected outcome. The algorithm must independently discover the patterns we are looking for. The main goal of UL is to explore and organise the data and identify key features or groups. Unlike SL, where we know the number and type of categories we are looking for, in UL, the number and nature of the results (e.g. the number of clusters of an issue) can be unknown and depend on the algorithm implemented and its parameters. We most commonly use SL for clustering, that is, grouping data into clusters based on their similarities (segmenting customers in marketing based on their purchasing behaviour, grouping photos according to visual similarities or classifying types of activity in sensor data like walking and running); dimensionality reduction, that is, simplifying data so that the most important information is retained with fewer variables (compressing data for visualisation in 2D or 3D or preparing data for further processing by other algorithms) and anomaly detection, that is, identifying unusual data that is different from the majority.

We also use it for detecting errors, fraud and unusual events (detecting bank fraud based on unusual transactions, finding defects in production lines or monitoring IT systems for suspicious activity). Another is association rules, that is, discovering relationships between elements in data (shopping basket analysis in shops, e.g. customers who buy milk often also buy bread or rolls, and recommending products based on specific shopping patterns). The last is temporal data clustering, that is, discovering seasonal patterns or trends in data that change over time (user behaviour analysis in mobile apps or temporal segmentation in financial analysis). The most popular UL algorithms in the field of clustering are clustering using K-means (Ikotun et al. 2023), which groups data into a finite number of clusters by minimising the distance of the data from the centre of the cluster; hierarchical clustering (Ghosal et al. 2020), which creates a hierarchy of clusters in the form of a tree (dendrogram); and density-based spatial clustering of applications with noise (DBSCAN (Bajal et al. 2022)), which groups data based on their density and deals well with outlier points in the dataset.

Dimensionality reduction is the process used to reduce the dimensionality of a dataset; taking multiple features and presenting them as fewer features are what comprise the principal component analysis (Hasan & Abdulazeez 2021) (PCA) algorithm, which compresses data while retaining the principal components (axes of greatest variance); t-distributed stochastic neighbour embedding (Balamurali 2023) (t-SNE) visualises multivariate data in 2D/3D preserving local structures and uniform manifold approximation and projection (Armstrong et al. 2021) (UMAP) is an alternative to t-SNE that is faster and better preserves global data structures. In the field of anomaly detection, there are the autoencoding algorithm (Qian et al. 2022), where NN compresses the data and reconstructs it, and the isolation forest algorithm (Batalov et al. 2024), a DT algorithm that isolates outlier data. In the field of association rules, there are the apriori algorithms (Santoso 2021), which look for frequent patterns in transactional data (e.g. which products are frequently bought together), and the frequent pattern growth (FP-growth) algorithm (Lakshika & Caldera 2022), which is an efficient alternative to the apriori algorithm but better able to deal with large datasets.

Advantages of SL include flexibility, the ability to work on any unlabelled data, being exploratory, discovering new patterns without the need for prior knowledge of the data, being economical and no need for manual labelling of data. Disadvantages include difficult interpretation of results, lack of "valid" results, which makes it difficult to evaluate the results obtained, sensitivity to parameters, significant variation in algorithm results depending on parameters (e.g. number of clusters), problems with large data and some computationally expensive algorithms (e.g. hierarchical clustering). We use algorithms based on UL for genome analysis to detect new disease subtypes, patient clustering based on similarities in medical data, customer segmentation (e.g. by purchasing behaviour or order value) and pattern analysis in shopping baskets. We also use UL to detect abnormal activity in computer networks, log analysis to detect attacks or clustering of stars in astronomy and analysis of biological data (e.g. genotypes and species populations). UL is a powerful tool for exploring unlabelled data to discover hidden patterns and structures. Its use is crucial in situations where data is not sufficiently understood or labelled.

RL (Gu et al. 2022) involves coaching an agent to make decisions in the environment so as to maximise long-term reward. The agent learns through trial and error, based on feedback in the form of rewards (or punishments) for its actions. The key elements of RL are the figure of the agent and the learning system that makes decisions. Another is the environment, the setting in which the agent operates (e.g. a game, robot or simulation). Another element is the state, the representation of the current situation in the environment that the agent observes; action, the action the agent can take in a given state; reward, the feedback from the environment indicating how good the agent's action was; policy, the agent's strategy for determining what actions to take in different states; and value function, which assesses how good a situation (state) is in terms of future rewards. How does RL work? The first step is to interact with the environment. The agent observes the state of the environment, takes an action, receives a reward and moves on to the next state. The next state is exploration. The agent tries new actions to learn more about the environment and selects the best-known actions to maximise the reward. The next goal is nothing more than maximising the cumulative reward over the long term, even if this means short-term sacrifices.

We distinguish between two RL models. One model is free RL (Gu et al. 2022), where the agent does not know the environment model (i.e. it does not know how its actions affect the states), that is, Q-learning (Clifton & Laber 2020) and deep Q-networks (Özalp et al. 2020) (DQN). Another model is based on RL (Zhu & Zhang 2021), where the agent builds a model of the environment to predict future states and rewards, for example planning using the Monte

Carlo tree search algorithm (Świechowski et al. 2023). The most important RL algorithms are Q-learning (Clifton & Laber 2020), an array algorithm where the agent learns a function Q(s, a) which evaluates the value of an action in a given state; deep Q-learning (Skolik et al. 2022) (DQL), an algorithm that uses NN to approximate Q-functions for large state spaces; policy gradient (Zhang et al. 2020), which directly optimises the agent's policies (e.g. REINFORCE and PPO – proximal policy optimisation); and actor-critic (Chen & Goldberg 2020), which combines policy (actor) and value function (critic) approaches for better learning. We use algorithms based on RL for automatic control in video games, robot control (e.g. walking and grasping objects), control of autonomous vehicles, resource management in cloud computing, optimisation of telecommunication networks, algorithmic trading, investment portfolio optimisation, production planning or urban traffic optimisation. Advantages of RL include the ability to solve complex sequential problems.

The algorithm learns from experience, without the need to label data, and can operate in dynamic environments. Disadvantages include high data and computation requirements, problems with exploration in very large state spaces and difficulty in selecting appropriate rewards (can lead to undesirable outcomes). RL is a key tool in AI, especially where decisions need to be made sequentially and should be optimised over time.

AI consists of several key elements. The basic element from which AI learns is data (e.g. text, images or sounds). They should have quality and be accurate, complete and error-free. They should have an appropriate structure. It can be tables and numbers, for example Excel sheets, that is structured data or text, images and sound–video material, that is unstructured data. There should be as much of it as possible. A large amount of data is crucial for effective model training. They should be diverse, that is, cover a wide range of cases, so that trained models work universally. For SL, the data must be appropriately labelled (e.g. labels in classification). In addition, they must reflect reality to avoid errors and biases in the model and be current and fresh to reflect current trends in science and life. Well-prepared data is the key to effective learning AI.

Another element of AI is the algorithms used: Principles and mathematical models that enable data processing (e.g. NN and DT). They are characterised by the type of learning (SL, UL and RL). The main ones are LR, an algorithm for predicting numerical values; KNN for similarity-based classification; NN, models inspired by the human brain or RF, a combination of DT for greater accuracy, precision and decision-making. The main features of AI are scalability, the ability to work with large datasets, computational complexity that requires sufficient computing power and adaptability that allows personalisation of parameters (e.g. hyperparameters). We apply AI in computer vision (CV), natural language processing (NLP (Boorugu & Ramesh

2020)), recommendation systems or forecasting. Good algorithms are the basis of good intelligent systems!

Another element that makes up AI is computing power. There is no creator of the definition of AI computing power. It arose spontaneously with the development of computer engineering, which was developed by companies such as Intel, IBM and NVIDIA, for example. AI computing power is the ability of an AI system to process and analyse data to perform specific tasks. It is strongly dependent on hardware resources (e.g. CPU (Alaei & Yazdanpanah 2024) – central processing unit, GPU (Alaei & Yazdanpanah 2024) – graphics processing unit, TPU (Jouppi et al. 2023) – tensor processing unit or NPU (Li et al. 2024) – neural processing unit) and the optimisation of algorithms and models. The high computing power allows complex models to be trained and complex calculations to be performed quickly.

Another component of AI is its models. GPT (Yenduri et al. 2024) is an advanced language model which generates natural text, supports various world languages, is used in chatbots, translation and creative writing and adapts responses to the context of the conversation. BERT (Zhou et al. 2023), an NLP model developed by Google, analyses the context of words in a sentence. It is used in Internet search engines and text classification systems. DALL-E (Zhou et al. 2023), a model that generates images from a textual description, combines NLP with computer graphics and creates realistic and abstract visualisations. Stable Diffusion (Dehouche & Dehouche 2023), an AI system for generating high-quality images with open-source code which enables a variety of applications, such as digital art, converts textual descriptions into graphics. Claude (Cartwright et al. 2024) is a language model from Anthropic, designed with a focus on safety and AI ethics, and is useful for conversations and content generation. Midjourney (Chiu 2023), an AI art generation tool with a unique style, is popular with graphic designers and digital artists and uses visual processing algorithms. AlphaFold (David et al. 2022), a model for predicting protein structures from amino acid sequences, is a revolution in molecular biology, accelerating drug and life science research. AlphaGo (Miao et al. 2023) is an AI model from DeepMind that beat the champions in the game of Go. ASI (Strelkova 2017) is currently mainly hypothetical. The concept originated alongside the idea of AGI, where ASI refers to AI that surpasses human intelligence in all areas. A. Turing and I.J. Good predicted the possibility of an "intelligence explosion" in the 1950s, where AI could improve itself independently. ASI remains a topic of philosophical, ethical and technological debate, and its potential implications are often discussed in literature and in analyses about the future of AI, for example, by Elon Musk and Nick Bostrom. It may require strict control, as, if mismanaged, it could pose a threat to humanity.

The fifth essential component of AI is software. Software is the set of instructions and data that control the operation of a computer, device or system.

It can take the form of applications, operating systems, drivers or tools. It is divided into system software (e.g. Windows and Linux), application software (e.g. word processors) and programming software (e.g. compilers). At the core of AI are libraries (collections of ready-made functions, classes or modules that developers can use in their projects) and frameworks (ready-made components, libraries and tools, eliminating the need to write source code from scratch), such as TensorFlow (Developers 2022) (a comprehensive ML framework which supports deep learning models), PyTorch (Imambi et al. 2021) (a flexible and popular framework used in deep learning research) or Scikit-learn (Kramer & Kramer 2016) (a framework equipped with tools for classical ML). Other AI frameworks include Keras (Manaswi & Manaswi 2018) (used to build NN and works using TensorFlow), Hugging Face Transformers (Jain 2022) (a framework specialising in NLP models such as GPT or BERT), MXNet (Chen et al. 2015) (a scalable framework for deep learning, which supports multiple programming languages), Caffe (Danopoulos et al. 2018) (an efficient framework for convolutional networks) or FastAI (Howard & Gugger 2020) (a high-level API[1] over PyTorch, used for simplified deep learning).

Another component of AI is infrastructure. AI infrastructure is the set of technological resources needed to create, train and deploy AI models. It includes hardware (GPUs, TPUs, servers and cloud computing); software (frameworks, data and model management tools); data (datasets for training and testing models) and management (systems for model versioning, orchestration and monitoring). AI model versioning systems are the process of managing different versions of models as they are developed, trained and deployed. They help track changes to models, experiment with different parameter settings, compare results and maintain control over the model life cycle. Versioning involves storing models, where each model version is stored with a unique identifier such as a name or version number; tracking model performance by recording settings and hyperparameters, such as architecture, training data or number of epochs and comparing results, which allows the performance of different versions of models to be evaluated on a test basis. Orchestration in the context of AI is the process of managing and co-ordinating the different stages of the AI model life cycle, such as data collection, model training, testing, deployment and monitoring. The aim of orchestration is to automate and optimise these activities to make the processes more consistent, efficient and repeatable. Elements of orchestration in AI include pipeline[2] automation, that is creating automated workflows that manage the entire sequence of activities (e.g. data ingestion, model training and deployment); data management, that is collecting, storing and preparing data in a way that allows it to be easily used by the various components of the model; integration with systems, the combination of different tools and services such as ML frameworks, databases, computing servers or cloud platforms; monitoring and version management, tracking results, metrics and logs and controlling the versions of the models used to ensure stability and efficiency over time. With versioning, it is easier to deploy models in a production environment and roll back to earlier versions if there are problems with the new ones.

Another important component is AI operating rules and ethics. AI operating rules and ethics refer to a set of principles and guidelines to ensure that AI systems are developed, deployed and used responsibly, fairly and safely. AI ethics seeks to address issues of bias, privacy, transparency, accountability and social impact. This includes several key areas such as security and reliability, transparency and explainability, impartiality and fairness, privacy and data protection, accountability and oversight, sustainability and social impact and legal compliance.

Safety and reliability of AI (Gnad et al. 2024) are key aspects in the development and deployment of AI systems to ensure that AI performs as expected, is fault-tolerant and does not pose a threat to users or society. These issues include both technical and ethical aspects. AI security refers to the protection of systems from threats and attacks which may affect their operation or use in ways that are not intended. In this context, a distinction is made between resilience to attacks (AI systems need to be protected against various forms of attacks such as adversarial attacks, which manipulate input data to deceive the AI model and force it to make wrong decisions; malware (e.g. malware) which can affect the performance of the AI system; and data attacks, modifying input data to manipulate the results generated by the AI). AI models should protect the privacy of the data used in the learning and inference processes. It is important to ensure that personal and sensitive data are adequately protected from unauthorised access and safeguard the training process. AI should be resistant to unintended changes during the training process so that the model is not vulnerable to manipulation which could affect its ability to make appropriate decisions. AI reliability refers to the ability of an AI system to operate in a predictable, stable and efficient manner over a long period of time. AI models should be able to operate consistently, without unexpected errors or failures, and be stable. For example AI systems in autonomous vehicles must operate reliably to avoid accidents. Before deploying AI in production, the systems must undergo thorough testing to ensure they work as expected. Testing includes testing on data from different sources to see how AI handles a variety of cases and simulations of different failure scenarios or unpredictable conditions to see how AI responds to emergencies. It is important to implement mechanisms which monitor and assess the potential risks associated with AI operations. This applies to both activities during training and model operation in a production environment. AI models need to operate in a predictable manner, especially in key areas such as medicine or law, where AI-based decisions have a major impact on people's lives. Models should be able to explain their decisions and predictions. Different approaches and technologies are used to ensure safety and reliability and model verification and validation, that is regular testing and auditing of AI models to detect potential errors or anomalies.

They are training on different datasets – using diverse, well-chosen datasets to train models to reduce the risk of errors and overspecialisation on one type of data – use of attack protection systems, that is, using methods such as defence against adversarial attacks, anomaly detection and real-time monitoring; safe and ethical programming practices, using good programming practices such as unit testing, version management, performance monitoring and proper documentation of code; and compliance with regulations and standards, adhering to international standards and regulations such as General Data Protection Regulation (GDPR) for personal data protection or ISO/IEC 27001 for information security management. Ensuring the security and reliability of AI is crucial if the technology is to be used responsibly and serve society without uncontrollable risks. It must be designed to be safe and reliable in a variety of environments, especially where decision-making can have serious consequences (e.g. autonomous vehicles and medicine).

The final and not insignificant component of AI are rules and ethics. This is a set of principles, guidelines and standards which aim to ensure that the development and deployment of AI technology are done in a responsible, fair, transparent and safe manner, respecting human rights and social principles. As AI becomes more and more present in everyday life, its ethical aspects are crucial in ensuring that it not only brings benefits but also does not introduce negative consequences such as prejudice, discrimination or threats to privacy.

Key ethical principles (AllahRakha 2024) related to AI have been developed. Impartiality and fairness: AI should be designed and used in a way that is free from biases which could lead to discrimination based on race, gender, religion, sexual orientation, nationality or other characteristics. AI models must be trained on representative, diverse datasets so as to minimise the risk of bias. So, at the very least, AI-based recruitment systems should be free of bias against women or minorities, and predictive algorithms for court cases must not favour any social group. Transparency and explainability: Users of AI systems should be able to understand how and why the system makes a particular decision. AI models, especially those used in critical areas like health or law, must be explainable so that users can understand the basis for their decisions. Privacy and data protection: AI must adhere to privacy principles, ensuring that personal data is collected, stored and used in a way that complies with legislation, such as the GDPR in the European Union. In addition, AI systems should apply privacy-preserving methods, such as data anonymisation, at least in medicine. Accountability and oversight: Developers, operators and users of AI systems should be held accountable for their performance, including the consequences resulting from errors or incorrect decisions made by AI. It is also important that AI systems are supervised by humans, especially when making high-impact decisions. Security and reliability: AI systems must be designed to be secure, reliable and stable. They must be resilient to attacks, failures or other threats that could lead to unintended and dangerous outcomes. Sustainability and social impact: The development and deployment of AI should take into account long-term impacts on society, including on the labour market, education and social justice. AI technologies should not lead to increased inequality or social exclusion. Lastly, legal compliance: AI should be developed and applied in compliance with applicable laws and regulations. This includes data protection laws as well as security regulations and technology standards. The principles of AI ethics are supported by a set of "Asilomar AI Principles" (Morandín-Ahuerma 2023), developed by experts in 2017, which places an obligation on AI developers to ensure that the technology is developed responsibly, safely and in the interests of humanity. They are also supported by the "Ethics Guidelines for Trustworthy AI" (Reinhardt 2023). Guidelines were developed by the European Union in 2019 to create an ethical framework for AI. They include seven core principles such as transparency, accountability, non-discrimination and sustainability. Another initiative is the IEEE Global Initiative on Ethics of Autonomous and Intelligent Systems. Established by the Institute of Electrical and Electronics Engineers (IEEE) to develop ethical principles for the development and deployment of autonomous and intelligent systems, including AI, it was launched in 2016 to address the growing challenges of developing technologies which have the potential to change the way we live and work, including in areas such as robotics, AI, autonomous vehicles and AI-based decision-making systems.

AI ethics help to ensure that this technology is used in a way that is not only innovative and effective but also protects people and society from negative impacts. Adhering to ethical standards in the development of AI is key to ensuring that this technology will positively impact the future while preserving humanity's core values.

The key components of AI are not only ML, SL, UL and RL, as described earlier, but also NLP (Chung et al. 2023) and CV. NLP is a field of AI that deals with enabling computers to understand, analyse, generate and interact with natural language spoken by humans. NLP combines elements of computational linguistics, statistics, ML and AI to create systems which can process texts or speech in a way that approximates human understanding of language.

The main goals of NLP are to understand natural language, that is, to enable computers to understand the meaning of words, sentences and context in a given text – for example distinguishing homonyms (words that have different meanings depending on the context), analysing sentiment in reviews, generating language and producing texts that sound natural and make sense in a given context. Examples include generating responses in chatbot systems or machine translation. Machine translation is the automatic translation of text or speech from one language into another, such as Google Translate. Speech recognition enables computers to understand human speech and convert it into text. Examples include voice command recognition in voice assistants such as Siri (Kepuska & Bohouta 2018), Alexa (Buteau & Lee 2021) and Google Assistant (Tulshan & Dhage 2019). Information extraction is extracting key data from texts, for example name, location and date, which is useful for analysis, search or recommendation systems. The basic tasks of NLP are tokenisation, which is the division of text into smaller units such as words, sentences or phrases; lemmatisation and stemming, the processes of transforming words to their basic form (e.g. "dog" instead of "dogs"); named entity recognition (Jiang et al. 2016) (NER), detecting and classifying proper names in text (e.g. people, organisations and places); sentiment analysis, determining whether a text expresses positive, negative or neutral emotions; and paraphrasing and summarising text, generating shortened versions of long texts without losing relevant information. NLP is central to the development of modern communication technologies which enable machines to better interact with humans through language, changing the way we communicate with machines and how machines analyse and understand the world around us. CV (Szeliski 2022) is a field of AI that enables computers and machines to "see" and interpret images and videos in a similar way to how humans do. The aim of CV recognition is to enable machines to understand and analyse visual data, allowing them to recognise objects, understand scenes, track objects in real time and make decisions based on visual information. The main goals of CV are object recognition, identifying and classifying different objects in images or video (e.g. detecting people, animals, vehicles and everyday objects); image segmentation, dividing the image into different parts or segments to facilitate the analysis of individual objects or regions of the image (e.g. separating background from objects); object tracking, tracking the real-time movement of objects on video or in surveillance cameras (e.g. tracking the position of a moving vehicle); face recognition, identifying faces in images or video, which finds applications in security systems, user identification, etc.; text recognition (OCR), converting text in images or video into digital form, which is used in document scanning systems; and scene and context analysis, understanding the overall scene in an image – what objects are in it, how they are positioned and their interrelationships. Computerised image recognition is a key technology which has wide applications in today's AI systems, from medicine to transport, and its development is opening up new possibilities in different areas of life.

Applications of AI: Much has already been said about the many applications of AI, but for the sake of tidiness, a brief summary is provided. In medicine, the application of AI is revolutionising diagnosis, treatment and health management, increasing the precision, speed and efficiency of medical interventions. Key areas include diagnostic imaging, detecting diseases from X-ray images, computed tomography (CT) and magnetic resonance imaging (MRI), which contributes to the diagnosis of lung cancer, breast cancer, skin cancer or the analysis of diabetic retinopathy; personalising medicine, creating therapies tailored to the patient's genotype thanks to genome and BDA; AI-based medical assistants, chatbots and systems to support doctors' decisions by analysing symptoms and suggesting possible diagnoses; surgical robots, assisting operations through precise movements and real-time analysis (e.g. da Vinci system); health monitoring, where AI is applied to wearables (e.g. smartwatches) analysing data such as heart rate, sleep, stress levels and detecting early signs of health problems; accelerating clinical trials, data analysis and virtual simulations, which are speeding up the development of new drugs; disease and epidemic prediction, predicting the development of diseases based on historical and current data (e.g. epidemic models); and automation of medical records, speech recognition and text analytics to create medical records. AI in medicine reduces the burden on doctors and improves the accuracy of diagnoses and the accessibility of healthcare.

The use of AI in industry increases efficiency, automates processes and supports decision-making. Key areas include production automation, AI-assisted industrial robots for precision tasks such as assembly, welding, painting, real-time monitoring of production lines or fault detection; predictive maintenance, analysing machine data, predicting failures before they occur and minimising downtime; process optimisation, where real-time data analysis allows production parameters to be adjusted, reducing resource and energy consumption; supply chain management, demand forecasting, optimisation of logistics routes and inventory management; quality control, where AI-based vision systems detect product defects such as damage or dimensional inaccuracies; design and simulation, in which AI-assisted generative design accelerates the creation of new products; energy management, optimising energy consumption in factories and automatically controlling energy systems and worker safety, which comprises video monitoring to detect potential hazards at workplaces.

The use of AI in finance increases the efficiency of operations, reduces risk and supports decision-making. Key areas of AI use in finance include fraud detection, where algorithms analyse transactions in real time to detect suspicious activity and anomalies (e.g. data theft and money laundering); risk management, where large datasets are analysed to assess credit, investment and operational risks; algorithmic trading, where AI makes investment decisions in fractions of seconds based on market analysis and asset price forecasts; chatbots and customer service, where customer queries are automatically responded at banks and insurance companies (e.g. account management assistance); personalisation of financial services, where credit, investment and insurance offers tailored to individual customer needs are created; financial planning, where AI assistants advise clients on saving, investing and budget management; market data analysis, where financial reports, articles and trends are processed to anticipate market changes; and lastly, process automation, where back-office activities such as loan application processing and document verification are optimised.

The use of AI in marketing improves personalisation, automates processes and increases the effectiveness of marketing campaigns. Key areas are content personalisation, where AI analyses customer behaviour to tailor ads, emails and product recommendations; product recommendations, where algorithms suggest products based on purchase history, browsing and preferences; ad targeting, which is precise targeting of advertising campaigns to relevant audiences through analysis of demographic and behavioural data; data analysis and forecasting, AI analyses marketing data to predict trends, campaign effectiveness and potential customer needs; chatbots and customer service, which is automatically interacting with customers in real time, answering questions and supporting the buying process; content generation, creating advertising texts, social media posts or product descriptions using AI models; sentiment analysis, monitoring customer feedback on social media, reviews and surveys to measure reactions to products or campaigns; and campaign automation, the planning and execution of advertising campaigns without human intervention, such as the dynamic adjustment of budgets or schedules.

The use of AI in transport enhances safety, optimises operations and supports sustainability. Key applications include autonomous vehicles, AI enables self-driving cars, drones and trucks to move by analysing the environment and making real-time decisions; route optimisation, algorithms determine the shortest and most efficient routes, reducing costs and fuel consumption; fleet management, real-time vehicle monitoring, predictive maintenance and efficient route and delivery planning; traffic forecasting, analysing traffic data to predict traffic jams and dynamically adjust vehicle routes; safety systems, AI supports advanced driver assistance systems (ADAS) such as automatic braking, sign recognition or driver fatigue analysis; public transport, timetable optimisation, passenger flow management and automatic vehicle control (e.g. autonomous metro); logistics and warehousing, automation of parcel sorting, dynamic inventory management and real-time monitoring of shipments; and sustainability, CO_2 emissions analysis and optimisation of transport systems to reduce environmental impact.

IoT is the concept of a network of interconnected physical devices, equipped with sensors, software and technologies which enable data to be collected, exchanged and analysed over the Internet, without human intervention. The history of IoT begins in the 1980s, when computer and network technologies were developing. The term "IoT" was coined in 1999 by Kevin Ashton, a

British pioneer of the technology and co-founder of the Auto-ID Center at the Massachusetts Institute of Technology. Gartner identifies IoT as one of the top 10 technology trends, and Cisco predicts that 50 billion devices will be connected by 2020, representing a potential market of more than $14 trillion. Similarly, it's not just technology-focused companies such as Ericsson, Bosch and Siemens that are using IoT to promote their advanced technologies – media companies such as the BBC are researching and have plans to implement IoT as well. In short, we are on the threshold of the emergence of a "mega-market" with markets such as home and building automation and power generation.

The development of IoT has taken place in stages, driven by technological advances and the increasing demand for automation and intelligent solutions. The beginning of IoT was in the 1980s and 1990s. In the 1980s, the "Connected Devices Concept" (Kellokoski et al. 2014) was developed. The concept of "connected devices" is the foundation for the development of the IoT and emerged with the idea that everyday objects such as a washing machine, fridge and microwave oven could be equipped with sensors, communication modules and intelligence to exchange data and collaborate with other devices using the Internet.

The genesis of IoT is the consideration of connecting devices within different types of computer networks. It was initially concerned with industrial systems and machinery and was inspired by early automation projects and computer networks such as ARPANET (Hauben 2007). The first example of a "connected device" that started the IoT was the Coca-Cola vending machine at Carnegie Mellon University (Alaba 2024) that stood there in 1982. It was one of the first devices to be called "smart". The vending machine was connected to the Internet to monitor the stock and temperature of the drinks.

Key elements of the IoT concept are communication between devices, the use of sensors and the decentralisation of data. The assumption was made regarding the communication between the devices that they would exchange information automatically without human intervention, using network protocols such as TCP/IP (Kessler 2004) and later HTTP. It was also assumed that many different sensors would be installed in the devices, which could collect data from the environment, such as temperature, humidity, movement or the state of the device, and that data decentralisation would enable data to be processed not only on the main servers but also locally, which was the first step towards edge computing (Cao et al. 2020). M. Weiser in 1991 in his article "The Computer for the 21st Century" (Weiser 1999) introduced the idea of ubiquitous computing. He envisioned a world where computers would be invisible and blended into everyday objects, which is the basis for the emergence and operation of the IoT. K. Ashton in 1999 first used the term "IoT" while working on a project using radio-frequency identification (RFID) (Nikitin et al. 2007) to track goods in the supply chain. In the initial phase of IoT development, the scale of deployment was limited by the high cost of sensors, communication modules and network infrastructure. Lack of standardisation of data transmission protocols and computing power limitations were also a problem. The technologies of the 1980s and 1990s had limited capabilities for both data processing and storage. Developments in networking technologies, especially between 2000 and 2010, such as the spread of Wi-Fi (Atzeni et al. 2022) and GSM technology (Mir et al. 2019), enabled greater mobility and accessibility of IoT devices. The introduction of IP version 6 (Ipv6) allowed the support of a huge number of IP addresses, which was crucial for the mass integration of devices. During this time, the first smart devices appeared (Suarez-Tangil et al. 2013), such as Nest thermostats and lighting systems. The IoT has exploded between 2010 and 2020. The widespread availability of sensors that has occurred as a result of falling sensor manufacturing costs and miniaturisation has allowed the integration of IoT technology into many areas of science and everyday life. The development of cloud services (Qian et al. 2009) (cloud computing) has enabled large-scale storage and analysis of data from IoT devices, and the development of consumer and industrial applications has enabled the emergence of smart homes (Jiang et al. 2004), cars (Arena et al. 2020), wearable devices (Xue 2019) (wearables) and industrial monitoring and automation systems (Younan et al. 2020) (Industrial IoT, IioT). After 2020, IoT is all about integration with AI and BD. Real-time analysis of data from IoT devices allows for more advanced applications, such as predictive maintenance or the emergence and surveillance of SC (Halegoua 2020). The introduction of 5G technology (Shafi et al. 2017) has significantly increased data transmission speeds and reduced latency, opening up new opportunities for IoT, especially autonomous vehicles. Increased awareness of the security risks of IoT devices is leading to the development of more advanced data protection mechanisms, and IoT ecosystems such as SC, smart factories or healthcare systems enable data exchange without human intervention, which was a theoretical assumption. From the perspective of recent years, the key factors shaping the development of IoT are the miniaturisation and falling cost of components, the standardisation of transmission protocols and the increase in computing power.

Technological developments have enabled the implementation of the concept of “connected devices” in many fields. Key applications in industry and automation (IioT) are the monitoring and predictive maintenance systems mentioned earlier. Devices in industrial plants, equipped with sensors, monitor machine parameters (e.g. temperature and vibration), and, on the basis of the collected data, failures are predicted, and production downtime is thus reduced to a minimum. Thanks to IoT, production lines automatically adjust settings (optimise production), adapting to current conditions, which increases productivity and reduces the amount of “produced” waste. RFID technology allows real-time tracking of materials and products in the supply chain, thus eliminating bottlenecks. Emerging smart homes are equipped with energy management systems. Thermostats such as the Nest Learning Thermostat from Nest, the ecobee SmartThermostat with Voice Control from ecobee and the Honeywell T9 Smart Thermostat from Honeywell analyse user habits and automatically adjust the heating or cooling temperature to save energy. They are equipped with smart lighting systems. Philips Hue, LIFX or Nanoleaf systems allow light colour and colour temperature to be changed. Additionally, it is possible to control them via mobile apps or by voice using Amazon Alexa (Lopatovska et al. 2019), Google Assistant (Gupta 2018), Apple HomeKit (Davidson 2017) or Hue Bridge (Skoumpakis 2016). Developed household appliances such as fridges and washing machines are controlled remotely via mobile apps. Refrigerators themselves monitor stock levels, suggest purchases, or place orders on behalf of the user. In the field of transport and logistics, intelligent transport systems have been developed. Connected cars (Solanki & Dhall 2017) exchange data with road infrastructure (e.g. traffic lights) to optimise traffic flow and increase safety. IoT enables real-time parcel location to improve delivery and customer service, and autonomous vehicles use IoT to communicate with other vehicles and road infrastructure elements (V2X – vehicle-to-everything (Wang et al. 2019)). In healthcare (Healthcare IoT (Farahani et al. 2020)), wearables, smartwatches and fitness bands (e.g. Apple Watch and Fitbit) monitor heart rate, physical activity and sleep quality, sending data to doctors or health apps. Medical devices such as glucometers or blood pressure monitors send patient data directly to the doctor, making it easier to monitor health conditions, and IoT systems in hospitals monitor patients' vital signs in real time, allowing faster responses in emergency situations. In emerging SC, street lighting is being managed with street lamps equipped with motion sensors that only switch on when pedestrians or vehicles are present, reducing energy consumption. IoT sensors measure levels of air pollution, noise or humidity, providing the data needed to manage urban space and, for example, indicate available parking spaces, reducing search times and emissions. None of this would have happened without the rapid development of technology. The key ones are, of course, RFID, Bluetooth (Al-Shareeda et al. 2023) and Wi-Fi, but Ipv6 and 5G networks are also making their contribution. It is impossible not to mention cloud computing and edge computing.

"BD" (Sagiroglu & Sinanc 2013) is a term describing a collection of data so large, complex and dynamic that traditional methods of processing and analysis are insufficient. BD includes data from a variety of sources, such as social media, IoT sensors, financial transactions or medical data. The key aspects of BD characteristics can be discussed on the basis of the 5V concept (volume, variety, velocity, veracity and value) and the specifics of the data and technology.

Volume, or massive amounts of data, is a key dimension of BD. The volume of data generated worldwide is growing at a dizzying pace, driven by advances in technology, digitalisation, IoT, social media and many other sources. In 2020, it was estimated that the world generated 64.2 (Data 2020) zettabytes (ZB) of data. By 2025, this number is expected to increase to 181 ZB (1 ZB = 1 billion terabytes). The main sources of this data are the generation of data by billions of IoT devices (smart sensors, home appliances and vehicles). SC can generate petabytes of data per day from traffic monitoring, energy management and security systems. Social media such as Facebook, Instagram and YouTube process millions of photos, videos and comments every day. YouTube handles more than 500 hours of video uploaded to the platform every minute.

E-commerce platforms such as Amazon and Alibaba process hundreds of millions of transactions per day, generating huge volumes of data about customers, purchases, their preferences and payments. Huge volumes of data are generated by autonomous cars (generating up to 25 GB of data per hour from sensors and cameras). Smart energy meters provide millions of data points on energy consumption. Banks and stock exchanges generate real-time data from millions of transactions. A single imaging study (e.g. MRI) can generate gigabytes of data, and data from health monitors is transmitted in real time. Every day, more than five billion Internet users generate data through searches, downloads, use of apps or uploading content. This volume of data generates storage problems. Traditional data storage systems cannot cope with such large collections. Scalable solutions such as the Hadoop distributed file system (HDFS) (Polato et al. 2014) and cloud computing (e.g. Amazon S3 (Persico et al. 2016) and Microsoft Azure Blob Storage (Daher & Hajjdiab 2018)) are required. Processing such large datasets also requires distributed computing systems (e.g. Apache Spark (Salloum et al. 2016) and Google BigQuery (Bisong & Bisong 2019)). However, the main problem is the huge costs. Therefore, companies are investing a great deal of resources in infrastructure optimisation and management systems, that is, the use of indexing, cataloguing and search tools.

Variety (Abawajy 2015) (variety and diversity of data) in the context of BD refers to the wide range of data types and sources that organisations need to manage and analyse. It emphasises the diverse nature of data. These data can have different forms, formats and structures. The literature distinguishes between three main types of data formats.

They are structured, semi-structured and unstructured data. Each of these formats brings different challenges and their applications. Structured data, according to data processors, are the easiest to analyse. This is because they have a clearly defined structure and are usually stored in relational databases (Khan et al. 2023). They are characterised by the following parameters:

- they are organised in the form of tables, precisely rows and columns;
- each column in a table represents a specific type of data (e.g. number, text, date, currency and percentage);
- data can be processed using various languages such as SQL (Ikromovna 2023).

Examples of data include customer databases (name, address, telephone number or insurance policy), data from ERP systems (Kunduru 2023) (sales data and stock levels) and data coming from financial records (bank transactions and balance sheets). The big advantage of structured data is its ease of processing with traditional analytical tools and the high performance of queries and modifications. Essentially, the only limitation is the flexible storage of data that does not fit into a specific, predetermined structure.

Semi-structured data (Ryen et al. 2022) are not stored in typical tables but have a certain hierarchy or structure, which allows them to be organised and analysed. They are characterised by the following features:

- they are organised in a way that allows dependencies to be identified, but are not fully structured;
- the standards used for these data are JavaScript Object Notation (Durner et al. 2021) (JSON – often used in APIs and web applications), eXtensible Markup Language (Blagoveshchenskaya et al. 2022) (XML – used for data storage and exchange) and Ain't Markup Language (Joshi 2024) (YAML – a simpler alternative to JSON, used, for example, in configuration files).

Examples of data include system and server logs (event data stored in JSON format), application configuration documents or e-commerce product data (JSON files describing categories, prices and details of individual products). The advantages of semi-structured data are the ease of transferring data between systems and the ability to store complex structures. In contrast, they are limited by the need to use specialised tools to analyse them and the fact that they can be more time-consuming to process than structured data.

Unstructured data make up the majority of data in BD ecosystems. They lack a unified model, which makes their analysis the most challenging. They are characterised by the following features:

- no clearly defined data structure;
- require advanced analysis algorithms such as NLP or ML;
- are often simply stored in distributed file systems such as HDFS (Saraswat & Raj 2021).

TABLE 1.1 Comparison of data formats

DATA TYPE	*STRUCTURE*	*EXAMPLES*	*TYPICAL ANALYTICAL TOOLS*
Structured	Tables	SQL and Excel	MySQL (Darmawikarta 2007) and PostgreSQL (Viloria et al. 2019)
Semi-structured	Hierarchical	JSON and XML	MongoDB (Chuhan 2019) and Elasticsearch (Thacker et al. 2018)
Unstructured	No structure	Video, text and image	Hadoop, Spark (Salloum et al. 2016) and TensorFlow (Sanchez et al. 2020)

Examples of data include social media content (posts, comments, photos and videos), text documents (emails, reports, articles and scripts) and multimedia (videos, sound recordings, images or footage from city surveillance cameras or drones). The advantages of these data are their rich context and the amount of information they contain, and that they are a potentially valuable source of new insights. On the other hand, they are limited by the difficulty of storing and analysing them and the high demand for computing power and memory to process or analyse them.

Other specific data formats include data in binary formats, audio files (e.g. MP3 and WAV), video files (e.g. MP4 and AVI), image files (e.g. JPEG and PNG), geolocation formats, spatial data in formats such as GeoJSON or KML, machine log formats, logfiles from operating systems, applications and IoT devices and streaming data (continuous data format, e.g., from IoT sensors or monitoring systems).

Source: Own elaboration

In summary, the diversity of data formats is both a challenge and an opportunity (see Table 1.1). Adapting analytical tools to different types of data allows them to be used more fully to make better business, research or operational decisions.

Data sources in the context of BD come from different areas of life, business, technology or science. Traditional data sources are the classic sources that were used in data analysis even before the BD era. Data from business systems are customer databases (CRM) or data from enterprise resource management (ERP) systems. Financial data are payment card transactions, bank account statements, statements from official registers, statements from tax registers or statements from the population register database. They are characterised by being structured and are usually stored in relational databases. These data are of high quality and accuracy. Data from social media are in the broadest sense (Ronzhyn et al. 2023). Social media generates huge amounts of data that are a valuable source of information about the behaviours, preferences and opinions of its users. Examples of data include posts and comments on Facebook, Twitter and LinkedIn and photos and videos on Instagram, TikTok or YouTube. Product reviews on platforms such as Yelp or TripAdvisor are also relevant data for analysis. They are characterised by their unstructured nature (text, images and video), high rate of generation of new data and rich content as a source of marketing information for trend analysis. Machine data are data generated by devices, IoT systems and technical infrastructure. Examples of data include system logs (server and application logs and security logs from SIEM systems), IoT sensor data (data from sensors installed in smart homes and data from IioT systems) and data from mobile devices, such as GPS location data or app usage information. They are characterised by semi-structured or unstructured and high frequency of real-time generation. Multimedia data include images, audio and video recordings, which are a rich source of information, especially in visual or acoustic analyses. Examples of data include images and videos from CCTV surveillance, voice recordings (e.g. from customer service centres) and live broadcasts (e.g. streaming from sports events). They are characterised by being unstructured, require advanced specialised analysis methods (e.g. image processing and speech recognition) and have high storage and processing space requirements. Public and open data are nothing more than publicly available data made available by government organisations, institutions and other entities. Examples of public data are government data (demographic statistics), meteorological data, scientific data (research results and publications), datasets from research projects (e.g. genomes and astronomical observations) and open data (resources available on platforms such as data.gov and OpenStreetMap). They are characterised by their availability in different formats (structured and semi-structured). An open licence allows them to be used freely. Trade and e-commerce data are data generated in the purchasing, customer service and product management processes. Examples of data include customer purchase history in online shops, website traffic data or product reviews and ratings.

They are characterised by structured (e.g. prices and orders) and unstructured (e.g. reviews) data. They offer the possibility to analyse customer preferences and personalise offers. Geolocation data are data related to geographical location, used in spatial analyses. Examples of data include GPS tracks from mobile devices, traffic maps (e.g. Google Maps) or satellite data (e.g. Earth imagery and agricultural analysis). They are characterised by semi-structuring (e.g. GeoJSON (Setiyadi & Setiawan 2023) and KML (Marques-Cruz et al. 2024)). They are most relevant in navigation, logistics and urban planning.

Streaming data are real-time data generated by various sources on a continuous basis. Examples of streaming data include data transmissions from financial exchanges, video streams from surveillance cameras and telemetry data from IT systems. They are characterised by the need to use specialised technology to process them in real time (e.g. Apache Kafka (Raptis & Passarella 2023) and Spark Streaming (Rajpurohit et al. 2023)). The challenge with these data is the need to process it quickly and analyse large volumes of data in real time. Another important source of data is industry-specific sources. Data are generated in specific areas that have unique applications. Healthcare generates electronic medical records (EMR), diagnostic images (e.g. X-ray and MRI) and genetic data (DNA). Finance generates real-time stock market transaction data, credit risk assessment and market analysis. Law enforcement generates data from surveillance footage, forensic data or logs related to cybercrime. The diversity of data sources is both a challenge and an opportunity. It enables comprehensive analysis but requires the right tools and methodologies to realise its full potential. An important step in the management of BD is to identify the sources that are most valuable for the specific analytical or business objective set.

Velocity (speed in BD) refers to the speed at which data is generated, processed and analysed in BD systems. In the context of BD velocity, we distinguish among:

- data generation – discussed earlier;
- data transmission – the speed at which data is transferred to storage and analysis systems, often requiring high-bandwidth infrastructure;
- data processing – the ability to analyse data in real time (real-time processing) or near real time. Technologies such as Apache Kafka, Spark Streaming or Flink (Davidson & Ravindran 2021) allow data streams to be analysed on the fly.

Examples of BD applications requiring high velocity include analysis of banking transactions to detect fraud in real time, social media monitoring to catch trends or respond to PR crises and recommendation systems that analyse user behaviour at the moment of action (e.g. Netflix and Amazon). Velocity challenges include managing data processing speed, minimising latency and scaling systems to be able to handle the increasing speed of data generation.

Veracity (reliability of BD) refers to the credibility of the data collected and processed. It refers to the quality, accuracy and reliability of the data that is processed and analysed. In practice, veracity emphasises the need to deal with data inaccuracies. Data inaccuracy in the context of BD refers to errors, omissions or inaccuracies in datasets that can affect analysis results and decision-making. In BD, where data is collected from different sources in huge volumes, this problem is particularly relevant. Sources of data inaccuracy include human error, incorrect data entry (typos and wrong numerical values) or lack of standardisation in filling in fields (e.g. different date formats and different units of measurement); technical problems, such as equipment failure during data collection (e.g. missing sensor readings) and errors in systems that integrate data from different sources; incomplete data (missing values in databases), data collected for only part of the population or objects (e.g. geographical data omitting certain regions); information noise (redundant or irrelevant data that hinder analysis) and false information (e.g. erroneous entries in online sources); and diversity of data sources (data from multiple systems with different standards, formatting or quality), conflicts between data from different sources (different values for the same variable). The consequences of data inaccuracies are erroneous analyses and predictions (which can lead to the generation of inappropriate conclusions, consequently affecting decision-making), loss of trust (organisations using low-quality data can lose credibility in the eyes of customers, partners or the public), increased costs (data correction and cleaning processes are time-consuming and costly) and legal problems (inaccuracies in data can lead to violations of legislation, e.g. GDPR in the case of improper processing of personal data). Several methods have been developed to deal with data inaccuracy. The first is record keeping and standardisation. Introducing uniform formats for data (e.g. standard formats for dates and measures), another method is to develop guidelines for users entering data. The next is data validation, that is, verifying the correctness of data at the time of entry (e.g. checking value ranges and correctness of formats). Another method is automatic data consistency checking (e.g. duplicate detection) and data cleaning, that is, deleting or correcting erroneous records. We can also fill in missing data through modelling or estimation (e.g. data imputation techniques) and monitor data quality through regular data quality audits of the organisation. The last method is data integration and unification by using extract–transform–load (ETL) systems to integrate data from different sources using AI/ML tools to harmonise them (e.g. resolving conflicts between data). Data reliability in BD is crucial, as even very large amounts of data lose value if they are not precise or are subject to errors. In practice, this means using tools and methods to clean, validate and assess their quality.

Value: In the context of BD, the term "value" refers to the benefits that can be derived from the analysis of large datasets. The value of data refers to its usefulness in making decisions, solving problems or generating innovation. Data only becomes a valuable resource when it is properly processed, analysed and used to achieve specific business or scientific goals. There are several types of data values in BD. Strategic value enables organisations to develop strategies based on real data rather than intuition or estimates. The analysis of BD sets allows trends to be identified, future events to be predicted and decisions to be made on the basis of facts. An example of the value of strategic data is in business, analysing market data to forecast demand, identify new market niches or optimise processes. In public administration, it is possible to predict the impact of public policies, for example, in healthcare or education. An example of the value of economic data is cost reduction in logistics by helping to optimise delivery routes and reduce fuel consumption. By creating new products and services, companies can develop new offerings, for example personalised services based on customer behaviour analysis. An example of the value of operational data is that organisations can streamline day-to-day operations and improve operational efficiency. Real-time analytics allows responding to changes in the internal and external environment. The exemplary value of social data is improving quality of life and solving key societal problems, for example, by using data to monitor and predict epidemics or analysing environmental data to help tackle climate change. The exemplary value of innovation data is the source of inspiration for new technologies, business models and solutions. Data analytics is opening the way to creating products and services which were previously impossible. The development of AI models is based on large training datasets, and in Industry 4.0, the use of BD in combination with IoT is leading to process automation and increased efficiency. An example of the value of predictive data is forecasting future events by analysing past patterns and trends. Predictive analytics, that is, what products will be popular in a given season, and, in the case of services, predictive crime analytics enable the prevention of criminal incidents. The exemplary value of contextual data allows an in-depth understanding of the context in which an organisation, customer or society operates. Analysis of customer preferences allows the creation of personalised advertising campaigns, and urban traffic analysis helps to plan infrastructure. The exemplary value of global data enables global collaboration to address global issues. Global analysis of weather data makes it possible to predict the effects of climate change and plan remedial action, while the analysis of international data contributes to faster responses to health threats. In summary, the value in BD is multidimensional and depends on the ability of an organisation or individual to use data effectively. The key is to transform raw data into useful information and practical actions that deliver economic, operational and social benefits.

CS (Hussain et al. 2020) is the field concerned with protecting computer systems, networks, data and users from cyber threats. It is a key area in both the public and private sectors, especially in the context of the increasing number of cyberattacks and their potential consequences. Key areas addressed by CS are data protection (Yanamala & Suryadevara 2024) (securing data against unauthorised access, loss, leakage or modification); network security (Kumar 2015) (securing computer networks against unauthorised access, viruses and distributed denial of service (DDoS) attacks); application security (Thomas et al. 2018) (ensuring that software works as intended, without cybercriminals being able to exploit its vulnerabilities); identity and access management (Glöckler et al. 2024) (controlling who can access systems and data and how); incident management (Li et al. 2022) (identifying, analysing and responding to security breaches); cryptography (Sharma et al. 2022) (using encryption techniques to protect data confidentiality) and education and awareness (training employees and end users to minimise the risk of attacks such as phishing (Sharma et al. 2022)). The most common CS threats are phishing (attempts to defraud by impersonating trusted entities), ransomware (Beaman et al. 2021) (software that blocks access to data, demanding a ransom to unlock it), DDoS attacks (Kumari & Jain 2023) (overloading a network or system to make it inoperable) and software vulnerabilities (Aslan et al. 2023) (vulnerabilities exploited by hackers to gain access to systems).

1.2 NNS AND THEIR IMPACT ON SOCIETY

The impact of NNs on society in general is large and varied, covering both positive aspects of life and challenges. Key areas where NNs impact society are:

- the economy and the labour market: The impact of NN on the economy and labour market is large and diverse, encompassing both the benefits of technological advances and the challenges of adapting to a changing work environment. NNs contribute to process automation. Process automation results in increased efficiency (NNs enable the automation of complex processes in many sectors such as industry, finance or logistics), reduced costs (through automation, companies can significantly reduce operating costs by eliminating repetitive and routine tasks) and increased innovation (companies can introduce new products and services faster through advanced AI-based analytics). However, there are also challenges: Downsizing (automation of processes can lead to job losses, especially in low-skilled sectors) and inequality of access (smaller companies that cannot afford to implement advanced technologies can be pushed out of the market). Job creation: The development of NN-based technologies is leading to new professions: AI/ML engineer, data analysis specialist, AI systems architect and AI ethics and compliance specialist. It is also leading to the development of technology sectors. The growth of industries is related to software development, CS or data analytics. These industries are growing, increasing the demand for highly skilled workers. However, they also present challenges. Job growth is accompanied by a shortage of talent (the dynamic development of AI is creating an increasing demand for specialists, leading to difficulties in recruitment and competition between companies for the best employees) and a need for retraining (a large investment in education and training is required so that employees can adapt their skills to the changing requirements of the labour market). Changing labour market structure includes new business models (NNs allow companies to introduce innovative business models such as digital platforms based on data analytics and real-time services) and globalisation of the labour market (the use of AI allows companies to benefit from the global talent market through remote working and international collaboration). Challenges related to changes in the structure of the labour market include labour market polarisation (an increase in the gap between high-skilled and low-skilled jobs, leading to an increase in social inequality) and a loss of employment stability (AI-based flexible working models may lead to an increase in short-term contracts and contract work). Impact on different sectors of the economy: Manufacturing and industry have responded to AI through the emergence of smart factories. NNs enable the implementation of Industry 4.0 concepts such as automation of production processes, machine failure prediction or resource optimisation: Robotisation (AI supports the development of industrial robots that are increasingly precise and autonomous); commerce and e-commerce (by analysing customer behaviour and dynamic pricing); finance and banking (fraud detection and risk management) and agriculture (AI supports the optimisation of fertilisation, irrigation and crop protection by analysing sensor data and satellite imagery). In summary, NN in the economy = global economic consequences. Benefits such as increased productivity (thanks to AI, economies can increase productivity, which translates into GDP growth) or competitiveness (countries and companies investing in AI gain a competitive advantage in the global market) give rise to challenges: Differences in the level of development (countries with less access to technology find it difficult to compete with AI leaders) and the monopolisation of markets (the dominance of large technology companies in the development of NN can lead to reduced competition).

- Health and medicine: The impact of NNs on health and medicine is revolutionary. AI-based technologies are helping to diagnose, treat and manage healthcare in a more efficient and personalised way. NNs and AI are a big support for medical diagnosis: Medical image analysis (NNs are used to analyse X-rays, CT scans, MRIs or mammograms. These algorithms help detect lesions, such as cancerous tumours, with a high degree of accuracy), disease diagnosis (AI systems are used for the early detection of chronic diseases such as diabetes, heart disease or neurodegenerative diseases) and faster results (the automation of medical data analysis reduces the time needed for diagnosis, which is crucial in emergency conditions). The benefits of using AI in medical diagnosis are precision (NNs can achieve diagnostic accuracy comparable to or higher than that of specialist physicians) and early detection (AI helps identify diseases at an early stage, which significantly increases the chances of successful treatment). Challenges include reliance on data quality (algorithms require large amounts of high-quality data for training, which can be a challenge in regions with limited access to medical infrastructure) and errors in interpretation (in rare cases, algorithms can generate false positives or negatives, which can affect therapeutic decisions). Personalised treatment. NN and AI are used to predict drug response (NNs analyse a patient's genetic data to predict which drugs will be most effective), optimise therapies (AI helps tailor drug doses and treatment regimens to individual patients) and precision medicine (by analysing the genome and medical data, NNs enable the design of therapies tailored to specific patient characteristics). Benefits include increased treatment efficacy (personalised therapies are more effective because they take into account a patient's unique characteristics) and reduced side effects (AI helps avoid unwanted side effects by better tailoring medication). Challenges include implementation costs (personalising therapies requires advanced technology and analysis, which can be costly) and ethics and privacy (storing and analysing genetic data raises questions about patient safety and consent). Telemedicine and remote monitoring: The use of NNs and AI for remote diagnosis (NNs are used in mobile applications and telemedicine systems to pre-diagnose diseases based on symptoms provided by the patient), health monitoring (IoT devices such as smartwatches use AI to analyse biometric data) and support for underserved areas (telemedicine enables access to specialists for patients in remote regions). Benefits include improved accessibility (remote solutions allow more patients to be reached, especially in areas with limited access to doctors) and early intervention (real-time monitoring allows deterioration of health to be detected more quickly). Challenges include equity of access (lack of digital access in some regions can limit the benefits of telemedicine) and reliance on technology (problems with technology infrastructure can disrupt telemedicine systems). Research and development of new therapies: The use of NNs and AI leads to drug discovery (NNs speed up the process of finding new therapeutic substances by modelling chemical and biological interactions), disease modelling (AI supports the creation of disease simulations, allowing a better understanding of disease progression) and clinical data analysis (NNs analyse vast amounts of clinical trial data, allowing faster inference and identification of effective therapies). The benefits of using NNs and AI are speeding up research (research processes that previously took years can be reduced to months) and reducing costs (automating analysis reduces the costs associated with drug development). Challenges include biological complexity (modelling human biological processes with NN requires vast computational resources and accurate data) and regulation (introducing new AI-based therapies requires meeting strict legal and ethical standards). Healthcare management: The use of NNs and AI enables resource planning (AI helps optimise the use of medical resources such as hospital beds, staff or equipment), prediction of health trends (NNs analyse epidemiological data to predict potential disease outbreaks or healthcare needs) and support for physicians (AI-based systems can act as assistants, suggesting possible diagnoses or treatment plans). The benefits are operational efficiency (better management of resources translates into greater efficiency in the healthcare system) and reduction of errors (AI supports medical staff in decision-making, reducing the risk of errors). Challenges include staff adaptation (the introduction of AI-based systems requires training and a change in attitude of medical staff) and initial costs (the implementation of such systems involves high investment costs). In summary, NNs are revolutionising medicine and healthcare, bringing huge benefits in terms of diagnosis, treatment, research and management. At the same time, challenges such as implementation costs, ethical issues and technology availability require attention and appropriate solutions. In the long term, these technologies have the potential to significantly improve the quality of healthcare and increase life expectancy worldwide.

- Education: The impact of NNs on education is significant and covers a variety of aspects, from personalising learning to developing tools to support teachers and students. NNs, a key technology in AI, are introducing innovations that are revolutionising learning and teaching processes. Personalisation of teaching: Adaptive learning systems (NNs analyse a student's progress in real time and adapt content according to the student's needs, learning style and proficiency level); personalised learning paths (AI-based systems can suggest individual learning plans to students, taking into account their strengths and areas for improvement) and intelligent tutoring (virtual learning assistants provide guidance and materials in a way which is tailored to the student's pace and style). Benefits include more effective teaching (students learn faster and more efficiently because materials are tailored to their individual needs) and support for struggling students (AI systems help identify and support students with dyslexia, ADHD (Kalbfleisch & Banasiak 2008) or other learning problems). Challenges include a lack of equal opportunities (personalisation technologies may not be available in schools with limited budgets, exacerbating educational inequalities) and data dependency (the effectiveness of personalisation systems depends on the quality and quantity of data on students). Automated grading: Assessment of written work (NN can analyse essays and other written work for grammatical correctness, argument logic and style), online testing (AI algorithms assess answers to closed and open-ended questions, providing results in real time) and progress analysis (educational systems can automatically generate reports on student progress, making it easier for teachers to monitor performance). Benefits include time savings (automation of assessment allows teachers to focus on other aspects of teaching) and objectivity (algorithms minimise the risk of subjective assessments). Challenges include a lack of flexibility (AI may find it difficult to assess creative or unusual answers) and ethical dilemmas (assessment automation raises questions about accountability for possible errors in assessment). Accessibility of education: Real-time translation (AIs enable translation of educational content into different languages, making knowledge more accessible to people from different language backgrounds), support for people with disabilities (AI technologies offer tools such as speech recognition, subtitle generation or voice interfaces that facilitate learning for people with physical or sensory limitations) and distance education (AI-supported e-learning platforms enable learning anywhere, anytime). The benefits are equality of opportunity (AIs help to address geographical and social barriers to accessing education) and inclusion (students with different needs can use the same learning materials through appropriate adaptations). Challenges include access to technology (in developing countries, the lack of digital infrastructure limits the benefits of AI in education) and the need for technical support (technical support is needed, especially for remote learning). Teacher support: Lesson planning (AI systems can suggest teaching materials, exercises and teaching methods based on curriculum analysis), problem detection (AIs identify students with learning difficulties, allowing teachers to intervene quickly) and educational content creation (AI helps generate materials such as quizzes, presentations or interactive simulations). Benefits include relieving the burden on teachers (AI reduces the administrative and operational burden, allowing teachers to be more involved in the teaching process) and a better understanding of students (by analysing data, teachers can better adapt their teaching methods to the needs of the group). Challenges include a lack of technological experience (not all teachers are adequately prepared to work with advanced AI systems) and dependence on technology (over-reliance on AI can lead to a reduction in teachers' creativity and intuition). New teaching and learning methods: Simulations and VR (Fitria 2023) (VR and AI support the creation of realistic simulations that help students understand complex concepts, e.g. in physics, biology or history), educational games (NNs enable the design of games to support learning through engaging and interactive experiences) and artificial tutors (virtual learning assistants can teach lessons, answer questions and provide guidance). Benefits include student engagement (interactive teaching methods increase motivation and engagement in learning) and effective hands-on learning (simulations allow students to practically apply knowledge in a safe environment). Challenges include the cost of implementation (implementing modern technology in schools requires significant investment) and the risk of dehumanising education (excessive use of AI may limit direct interaction between students and teachers). Analysis of educational data: Prediction of success and problems (AIs analyse data on student performance, predicting the risk of educational failure and helping to prevent it), curriculum optimisation (AI algorithms analyse the effectiveness of different educational methods and content, suggesting improvements) and education research (AI supports pedagogical research by providing data on the effectiveness of different approaches). The benefits are better decisions (data help schools and teachers make more informed decisions about education) and increased efficiency (data analysis allows for better use of educational resources). Challenges include data privacy (storing and analysing student information requires special care in terms of data protection) and the complexity of interpretation (analytical results can be difficult to understand and apply in practice). In summary, NNs are revolutionising education by introducing modern teaching methods, supporting teachers and making knowledge more accessible. However, their implementation comes with challenges such as the need for adequate infrastructure, data protection and equal access to technology. In the long term, AI has the potential to make education more efficient, personalised and accessible to all.

- Entertainment and culture: The impact of NN on entertainment and culture continues to grow. The technology is changing the way cultural and entertainment content is created, distributed and consumed, opening up new opportunities for both creators and audiences. Content creation: Music and sound generation (NNs, such as generative models (Regenwetter et al. 2022) (e.g. GAN or RNN), are able to create new musical compositions tailored to specific styles, moods or user needs); text and script creation (AI supports the writing of film scripts, books or dialogue in video games, generating ideas or whole chunks of text); visual art (generative algorithms are used to create images, graphics or special effects in films, series and games) and video production (AI automates the process of editing films, creating trailers or generating realistic animations). Benefits include technology-enhanced creativity (creatives can use AI to experiment with new forms of art and entertainment) and lower production costs (automating many creative processes lowers costs, allowing projects with limited budgets). Challenges include authenticity (the question arises as to whether AI-created works can be considered "real" art) and intellectual property (generating content from existing works raises copyright controversies). Content personalisation: Content recommendations (NNs drive recommendation algorithms on streaming platforms such as Netflix, Spotify or YouTube, suggesting content based on user preferences); personalised gaming experiences (AI analyses a user's play style and adjusts the difficulty level, storyline or opponents in video games) and interactive stories (NNs enable dynamic stories that change based on user decisions). Benefits include better customisation (users receive content that better matches their interests, increasing engagement) and audience satisfaction (personalisation improves the user experience, making the time spent consuming content more valuable). Challenges include information bubbles (algorithms may limit the variety of content, offering only what matches a user's existing preferences) and privacy risks (personalisation requires analysis of user data, which may raise concerns about its protection). Interactivity and immersion: AR and VR (NNs support the development of realistic virtual worlds, interactive experiences and cultural applications); realistic game characters (AI allows the creation of non-playable characters (NPCs) that behave in a more human-like manner and react to the player's actions) and interactive simulations (in museums or exhibitions, AI allows visitors to interact with virtual guides or exhibits). Benefits include increased immersion (AI allows to create more engaging and realistic experiences in games, films or museums) and immersion in education and entertainment (interactive content allows to combine fun and learning, such as in the form of educational games). Challenges include the high cost of the technology (development and implementation of advanced VR and AR applications can be costly) and accessibility (not every user has access to the hardware to use such technologies). Automation in the entertainment industry: Production management (AI optimises production processes in the film and music industry, e.g. shooting schedules, resource distribution or crew management), trend prediction (algorithms analyse market data and predict what genres of films, songs or games will be popular in the future) and marketing optimisation (NNs analyse consumer preferences and help create more effective promotional campaigns). The benefits are operational efficiency (automation saves time and resources) and better targeting (promotional campaigns become more effective by analysing user behaviour). The challenge is the risk of commercial dominance (the entertainment industry may focus on maximising profits at the expense of diversity and artistic value). New forms of art and culture: Generative art (AI makes it possible to create works of art that are unique and often impossible to achieve with traditional methods), artistic experimentation (AI opens up new paths for artists, making it possible, for example, to create interactive art whose reception changes in real time) and the digitisation of cultural heritage (AI helps to restore and preserve works of art and archives, for example, by reconstructing damaged paintings or films). Benefits include the development of creativity (AI inspires artists to explore new areas of creativity) and the preservation of cultural heritage (technology supports the protection and sharing of cultural assets for future generations). Challenges include ethical controversies (AI-created works may be perceived as less "authentic" compared to human creativity) and the impact on traditional art forms (the development of technology may result in the marginalisation of traditional creative methods). A change in the way culture is consumed: On-demand streaming (AI algorithms enable users to access content anytime, anywhere), interactive platforms (AI applications enable viewers to actively participate in content, e.g. by choosing the ending of a film or influencing the development of a storyline in real time) and online culture (NNs support the development of virtual concerts, exhibitions or theatre performances). The benefits are easier access (consumers can enjoy culture and entertainment at their convenience, regardless of location) and diversity of content (platforms offer a wide choice of content tailored to individual preferences). Challenges include the disappearance of traditional experiences (moving culture and entertainment to the digital space may lead to a reduced interest in traditional forms such as theatre or cinema) and algorithms versus diversity (personalisation of content may limit users' exposure to less popular forms of culture). In summary, NNs are significantly changing the entertainment and cultural industries, opening up new possibilities in the creation, consumption and management of content. They also introduce challenges related to ethics, accessibility and preservation of traditional forms of culture. Nevertheless, their potential to foster creativity, immersion and innovation makes them a key part of the future of entertainment and culture.

- Security and law: The impact of NNs on security and law is significant and covers a variety of aspects related to crime detection, data analysis, threat prevention and supporting legal systems. Use for crime detection and forensic analysis: Facial and object recognition (AIs analyse images from surveillance cameras, identifying suspects, vehicles or objects associated with crimes), crime pattern analysis (algorithms can analyse large datasets to detect recurring patterns of criminal activity) and data reading from audio and video recordings (AI supports transcription and analysis of evidence such as surveillance footage or wiretaps). Benefits include speed of response (automated data analysis speeds up the identification of potential threats and suspects) and juiciness (AIs can detect details that may be overlooked by humans). Challenges include the risk of errors (algorithms can make mistakes, e.g. misidentifying people based on their faces) and privacy (the mass use of facial recognition technology raises concerns about public surveillance). Threat prevention: Crime prediction (AI-based systems analyse historical data and predict the location and timing of potential criminal events), social media monitoring (AI identifies potential threats, such as planning terrorist attacks, by analysing public posts and content on the Internet) and CS (AI detects anomalies in network traffic, identifying attempted hacking attacks or intrusions into computer systems). Benefits include crime prevention (with early warning, preventive action can be taken) and increased public safety (AI systems allow faster response to potential threats). Challenges include profiling and discrimination (predictive models can unfairly focus attention on specific social groups) and false positives (incorrect inputs can lead to incorrect predictions). Legal systems support legal document analysis (AI automates searches of files, judgements and legislation, helping lawyers prepare cases), risk assessment (algorithms help assess defendants' risk of reoffending, which can influence parole or bail decisions) and legal translation (AI enables automatic translation of legal documents, which is particularly useful in international cases). The benefits are increased efficiency (automation of legal analysis saves time and costs) and increased accessibility of the law (AI helps citizens understand complex legislation). Challenges include a lack of context (algorithms may struggle to interpret complex legal cases) and the risk of bias (models trained on historical data may reflect existing biases). Support for crisis management: Large-scale incident monitoring (AI supports crisis management, e.g. by analysing data from drones, social media or real-time monitoring systems) and disaster risk assessment (NNs predict the impact of natural or technological disasters, supporting rescue efforts). The benefits are more efficient co-ordination of activities (AI enables rapid collection and analysis of data in real time) and minimisation of losses (early warning allows preventive action to be taken). Challenges include reliance on technology (over-reliance on AI in emergency situations can be risky in the event of system failure) and lack of transparency (decisions made by AI can be difficult for humans to understand).

- CS and data protection: Anomaly detection (Ais identify unauthorised access to systems, phishing attempts or other anomalies), encryption and data protection (AI supports the development of advanced security systems to protect against information leakage) and combating cybercrime (algorithms analyse network activity to help detect and neutralise botnets (Asadi et al. 2024), ransomware attacks (McIntosh et al. 2021) or phishing (Safi & Singh 2023)). Benefits include more effective protection of systems (AI can anticipate new cyber threats) and automation of responses to attacks (systems can take immediate action to minimise damage). Challenges include the race against cybercriminals (AI technology is also used by hackers, requiring constant adaptation of new anti-solutions), complexity of systems (extensive protection mechanisms can be difficult to manage). Ethical and regulatory aspects: AI rule-making (NNs support the analysis of the impact of regulation on security and privacy) and the ethical use of AI in law enforcement (technology helps to assess the potential impact of its use, such as algorithmic biases or restrictions on freedom). Benefits include better management of the technology (regulations can prevent abuse and promote responsible use of AI) and building public trust (transparent use of AI in law and security increases public acceptance). Challenges include regulation versus innovation (over-regulation can inhibit technology development) and global differences (lack of uniform international standards hinders effective cooperation). In summary, NNs have had a tremendous impact on security and law, bringing significant improvements to crime detection, forensic analysis, prevention and crisis management. However, their development also comes with challenges related to ethics, privacy and potential algorithmic biases. A balanced approach that realises the technology's potential while minimising the risks associated with its use is crucial.

- Society and ethics: The impact of NNs on society and ethics includes both positive and negative aspects. The technology is shaping interpersonal relationships, social values, behavioural models and moral principles, forcing us to rethink fundamental issues of responsibility, privacy, justice and human autonomy. Changing the dynamics of work and daily life: Automation of work (AIs contribute to the automation of processes in various sectors, which increases productivity but at the same time changes the structure of the labour market) and personalisation of services (AI enables customisation of products and services, which affects everyday consumer decisions). Benefits include increased convenience (AI automates routine tasks, saving time) and improved access to services (with personalised solutions, more people have access to education, healthcare and other services). Challenges include the dehumanisation of interactions (the increased role of technology in daily life can lead to a reduction in face-to-face human interaction) and the disappearance of traditional occupations (automation can lead to the social exclusion of people who are unable to adapt to new labour market requirements). Privacy and data security: Personal data analytics (AIs analyse huge amounts of data to create accurate user profiles) and monitoring and surveillance (AI is used to monitor online and offline activity, both commercially and by government agencies). Benefits include better services (user data allows for better-tailored offers and new product development) and increased public safety (surveillance technologies can help prevent crime). Challenges include invasion of privacy (unethical use of personal data raises serious privacy concerns) and risk of abuse (data can be used to manipulate or discriminate, such as in credit or recruitment systems). AI's ethics of accountability and decision-making (NNs are used in decision-making systems such as credit allocation, traffic management or medical diagnostics) and autonomous systems (AI controls autonomous vehicles, robots or military systems). Benefits include increased efficiency (automating decision-making processes speeds up tasks) and reduced human error (AI can minimise errors due to human fatigue or bias). Challenges include a lack of accountability (decisions made by AI may be difficult to attribute to a specific person or organisation) and moral issues (in critical situations, such as autonomous vehicles, AI may have to make moral decisions, choosing between two risks). Algorithmic biases: Historical data analysis (AI learns from existing data, which may include biases and inequalities) and recommendation and selection systems (AI is used to evaluate job candidates, allocate resources or predict behaviour). Benefits include an automated approach (AI can analyse data faster and more comprehensively than humans) and objectivity (potentially, AI can eliminate subjective human errors). Challenges include perpetuation of inequalities (algorithms learn from historical data, which can lead to reproduction of existing biases) and a lack of transparency (AI decisions are often difficult to explain, making it difficult to detect and correct errors). Manipulation and misinformation: Deepfake (Rana et al. 2022) (AIs can create realistic but fake images, videos and sounds) and content personalisation (AI tailors media content to users' preferences, which can be used to manipulate public opinion). The benefits are media innovation (deepfake and content personalisation have the potential to produce creative forms of entertainment and education) and faster information analysis (AI supports faster processing of large amounts of media data). Challenges include threats to democracy (manipulative content can affect election results and public opinion) and difficulties in detection (fake content is becoming increasingly difficult to distinguish from real content). Social inequality: Access to technology (NNs can be costly to implement, limiting their availability in less developed countries) and impact on education and the labour market (lack of access to technology education can exacerbate existing inequalities). Benefits include global development (AI technologies can accelerate the development of countries and regions that implement them) and new opportunities (AI creates new jobs and ways of education). Challenges include digital exclusion (those without access to technology can be marginalised) and concentration of resources (AI technology is often controlled by a few large corporations, increasing their influence on society). Transformation of social values: Virtual assistants and companions (AI is being used to create virtual characters to support people in daily life) and human–machine relationships (increasingly, people are interacting with machines on an emotional level). Benefits include emotional support (virtual systems can help lonely people or those suffering from mental disorders) and increased efficiency (AI can act as caregivers, therapists or counsellors). Challenges include loss of human relationships (AI development may lead to a decline in the value of traditional human relationships) and ethical issues (replacing humans with machines in emotional roles may be controversial). In summary, AIs have a profound impact on society and ethics, changing our daily lives, the structure of the labour market, the way we communicate and social values. While the technology brings many benefits, such as improved services, efficiency and innovation, it also poses serious ethical challenges, such as protecting privacy, preventing algorithmic biases and ensuring accountability for AI decisions. Striking a balance between realising AI's potential and protecting fundamental social and ethical values is key.

- Environment: The environmental impact of NNs includes both potential benefits and challenges. On the one hand, AI-based technologies (including NNs) can promote sustainable development, efficient resource management and conservation. On the other hand, their development and deployment come with significant environmental costs, including high energy consumption and carbon emissions. Supporting sustainable development: Climate change monitoring (AI-based technologies analyse satellite data, weather models and changes in ecosystems, supporting global warming research), energy optimisation (AI helps manage power grids, promoting the use of renewable energy sources and minimising energy losses) and water resource management (predictive algorithms help manage water efficiently, such as in agriculture and industry). Benefits include better forecasting and planning (AI identifies changes in the environment more quickly, enabling preventive action) and reduced resource waste (optimising processes leads to more efficient use of natural resources). Challenges include data availability (many regions lack adequate data to support effective AI models) and limited technology adaptation (implementing advanced technologies requires financial resources and infrastructure, which can be difficult in less developed regions). Biodiversity conservation: Endangered species monitoring (AI-based technologies analyse images and sounds from cameras and microphones in natural environments, identifying the presence and abundance of animals), anti-poaching (AI supports monitoring and alarm systems in protected areas, detecting illegal activities) and ecosystem rehabilitation (algorithms help plan activities to restore degraded environments). Benefits include faster response (AI enables early detection of threats to species and ecosystems) and precise data (AIs analyse vast amounts of data, providing detailed information on the state of the environment). Challenges include the cost of the technology (AI-based monitoring and analysis systems are costly to implement and maintain) and dependence on infrastructure (a lack of adequate infrastructure in ecologically important regions can limit the effectiveness of these solutions). High energy consumption and carbon emissions: Training of large models (training of advanced NNs, such as NLP or image generation models, requires huge computing power) and data centres (operation of infrastructure supporting NNs involves high energy consumption and greenhouse gas emissions). Benefits include infrastructure optimisation (deploying energy-efficient solutions in data centres can reduce environmental impact) and renewable energy development (AI supports the planning and deployment of green technologies such as photovoltaics and wind power). Challenges include AI's carbon footprint (training advanced AI models, such as GPT or DALL-E, generates significant CO_2 – for example one training of a large language model can emit as much CO_2 as a round trip on an intercontinental aeroplane) and a lack of transparency (data on energy consumption by technology companies are often not publicly available, making it difficult to assess environmental impact). Waste management and recycling: Recycling automation (AI recognises different types of waste on sorting lines, increasing recycling efficiency) and waste production forecasting (AIs analyse consumption and production data, helping predict waste volumes and plan for processing). Benefits include reduced pollution (automating recycling processes reduces the amount of waste going to landfills) and better resource management (AI-based forecasts support more efficient management of raw materials). Challenges include technological complexity (implementing AI-based systems requires advanced infrastructure) and the need for public education (technology alone will not solve the waste problem without changing consumer habits). Promoting green technologies: Renewable energy (AIs optimise the production and distribution of energy from renewable sources) and SC (AI supports resource management in cities, such as optimising street lighting or transportation systems). Benefits include sustainability (AI accelerates the deployment of environmentally friendly technologies) and emissions reduction (smart systems can reduce energy consumption and CO_2 emissions). Challenges include

> upfront costs (implementation of green technologies involves high investment) and regional inequalities (smart city development is mainly concentrated in developed countries). Environmental education and public awareness: Simulations and visualisations (NNs support the creation of models depicting the effects of climate change or environmental degradation) and educational platforms (AI helps create personalised educational programmes that raise environmental awareness). Benefits include a better understanding of environmental problems (AI-based technologies facilitate access to knowledge about the state of the environment) and motivation to take action (visualisations of climate change can inspire conservation efforts). Challenges include misinformation (technologies can also be used to spread false information about the state of the environment) and the complexity of the message (effective communication of environmental problems requires simplification of complex data, which can lead to shallowing of problems). In summary, NNs have great potential for environmental protection and sustainable development, from monitoring climate change to supporting green technologies. At the same time, their development comes at a high environmental cost due to high energy consumption and carbon emissions. A holistic approach is key to capitalising on AI's capabilities while minimising its negative impact on the environment. Implementing energy-efficient technologies, promoting renewable energy sources and raising environmental awareness are steps that can contribute to more sustainable development in the era of AI.

NNs are significantly impacting various aspects of society, bringing both benefits and challenges. In the economy and labour market, they automate processes, increase productivity and create new industries, but at the same time, they can cause job losses and growing inequality. In education, they make it possible to personalise learning and support students with special needs, although there are risks of technology dependency and digital exclusion. In medicine, they accelerate diagnostics, advance precision medicine and support research, but generate challenges with data protection and algorithmic errors. In culture and entertainment, they create new forms of creativity and personalise content, but can lead to the monopoly of big companies and the dehumanisation of the arts. In the context of security and law, they support the fight against crime and the optimisation of legal systems but come with privacy risks and ethical dilemmas. At the social level, they can eliminate human biases and promote equality, but, at the same time, reinforce algorithmic inequalities and manipulate public opinion. In the environmental field, they contribute to monitoring climate change and managing resources, although training AI models generates high energy consumption and CO_2 emissions. Ultimately, the responsible use of NNs requires global cooperation, thoughtful regulation and public education to ensure that the technology serves all segments of society, minimising the risk of exclusion, manipulation and environmental degradation.

1.3 CS IN AN ERA OF DYNAMIC TECHNOLOGY DEVELOPMENT

The dynamic development of technology, including AI, the IoT and cloud services, creates new opportunities for society, the economy and public administration. However, at the same time, it leads to CS challenges. The increasing number of cyberattacks, advanced hacking techniques and the global nature of cybercrime are making the protection of data and critical infrastructure a priority for institutions and companies. The main threats (today) in cyberspace are:

- Ransomware attacks: Ransomware involves encrypting the victim's data and demanding a ransom to unlock it. These attacks are becoming increasingly sophisticated, involving double extortion techniques in which criminals threaten to make the stolen data public if the ransom is not paid. Ransomware affects hospitals, schools, banks, governments and other organisations, often paralysing their operations for long periods;
- phishing and social engineering: Phishing is a technique for phishing for confidential information by impersonating trusted individuals or institutions. More advanced methods of social engineering, on the other hand, include spear phishing attacks that precisely target specific individuals or organisations. Users are often tricked into clicking on malicious links, opening infected attachments or providing credentials on fake websites;
- IoT threats: IoT devices, such as smart cameras, thermostats or industrial monitoring systems, are often manufactured without the appropriate security standards introduced by standards. Attacks on IoT can include taking control of devices, creating botnets (e.g. Mirai (Snehi & Bhandari 2021)) and disabling key systems in critical infrastructure;
- malware and advanced persistent threat (APT) attacks (Tatam et al. 2021): These are long-term and highly targeted attacks that aim to steal data, commit economic espionage or disrupt an organisation's

operations. Malware such as viruses, Trojans and rootkits (Sheikh 2021) often run in the background, remaining undetected by traditional protection mechanisms for long periods of time;

- DDoS attacks: These involve overloading the victim's network infrastructure by sending huge numbers of requests. Such actions can result in the temporary shutdown of Internet services, which particularly affects the e-commerce sector, online media or financial institutions;
- exploitation of zero-day vulnerabilities: Zero-day vulnerabilities are previously unknown vulnerabilities in software that have not yet been patched by the manufacturer. Criminals exploit these vulnerabilities to launch attacks on IT systems before the relevant security patches are in place;
- digital identity theft: Cybercriminals are increasingly focusing on the theft of personal data, which can be used to carry out fraudulent activities such as loan phishing, online ordering or bank account hacking;
- deepfake and information manipulation: The development of deepfake technology makes it possible to create realistic but fake audio and video content that can be used to disinform, blackmail or influence public opinion, such as during elections;
- threats to critical infrastructure: Critical infrastructures such as power grids, water supply, transport or financial systems are increasingly being targeted by cyberattacks. Examples include attacks on power plants (e.g. the Stuxnet virus, which was used to hit Iran's nuclear programme) or disruption of refineries;
- insider threats: Insider threats can come from employees who intentionally or accidentally disclose confidential information or introduce threats to systems. They often result from disgruntlement, negligence or lack of security knowledge;
- cyber espionage and cyberwarfare: States and government-sponsored groups are increasingly using cyberspace for espionage and warfare. Attacks of this type include the theft of state secrets, disruption of military systems and destabilisation of the opponent's economy.

In summary, the development of cyber threats requires constant adaptation of protection methods and investment in new protective technologies and education. Rapid response to threats, monitoring of systems and international cooperation are key to protection in a rapidly changing technological environment.

International strategies for increasing the level of CS are:

- user education and awareness: Regular employee training on cyber threats and the principles of safe use of IT systems should be standard in every organisation. This includes learning how to recognise phishing, manage passwords and respond to suspicious activity. In turn, countries and organisations should run information campaigns that, by raising public awareness of cyber threats and promoting basic security principles such as using strong passwords and keeping software up to date, will increase the level of CS. Simulations of, for example, phishing attacks and tests allow us to assess the preparedness of employees and identify areas requiring a response;
- use of advanced technologies: Security systems such as firewalls and IDS/IPS intrusion detection and prevention systems will allow network traffic to be monitored and potential threats to be detected in real time. AI and NNs can analyse large amounts of data, identify unusual patterns in network traffic and automatically respond to threats. These are particularly useful methods to combat zero-day attacks and other advanced attack methods. The use of strong encryption algorithms (e.g. AES and RSA) protects data during storage and transmission, minimising the risk of interception by unauthorised parties;
- implementation of security policies: Organisations should introduce requirements for the use of strong, unique passwords and for changing them regularly. The use of password managers further enhances the security of systems. Applying the principle of least privilege restricts access to data and systems to only those who need it as part of their job duties. Policies on the use of private devices at work such as bring your own device (BYOD) should include requirements for securing them, such as installing antivirus software or using VPNs;
- international cooperation: Joint initiatives and agreements and cooperation among states, international institutions (e.g. NATO and EU) and the private sector enable faster responses to threats and exchange of information on new attack techniques. International security standards, such as ISO/IEC 27001, help to create consistent protection policies and build trust between partners;
- penetration tests and security audits: Regular penetration testing (simulated attacks on IT systems) allows potential vulnerabilities to be identified and remediated before they are exploited by cybercriminals. Checking, as part of compliance audits, that the organisation complies with applicable regulations and standards, such as

GDPR, NIST or PCI DSS, helps avoid penalties and increases the level of data protection;

- incident response and crisis management: Every organisation should have an incident response plan in place and tested, which includes identifying the threat, notifying the relevant people and restoring systems. Also, every organisation should have incident response teams (e.g. CSIRT) in place. This allows for quick and effective crisis management in the event of cyberattacks;
- investing in research and development: The development of new solutions, such as quantum encryption (Ali et al. 2024) or secure operating systems (Jaeger 2022), significantly increases the level of protection against new threats. Meanwhile, cooperation with research centres supports the development of protection technologies and the creation of new methods to detect and combat cyber threats;
- the use of cloud solutions: Cloud services offer advanced security features such as data redundancy, encryption or threat detection systems. However, using them requires conscious data management and choosing trusted providers. Regular back-ups in a local or cloud environment allow data to be quickly restored in the event of an attack, such as ransomware;
- network segmentation and microsegmentation: By dividing the IT infrastructure (segmentation) into separate segments, the impact of potential attacks can be reduced, and the risk of lateral movement of threats can be reduced. By implementing more precise control of traffic within the network (microsegmentation), critical resources can be protected even in the event of a security breach;
- promoting a culture of security within the organisation. Management should promote a culture of security, actively support data protection initiatives and set priorities in the area of CS. Introducing reward programmes for responsible security behaviour, such as reporting potential threats, can increase employee commitment to protecting the organisation.

In summary, effective strategies to enhance CS require a comprehensive approach, combining modern technology with education, standardisation and collaboration. Organisations should continuously adapt their security strategies to the rapidly changing technological environment and continuously monitor and improve their security systems.

Public institutions play a key role in building a secure cyber environment at the national and international levels. Their tasks include creating regulations, monitoring threats, responding to incidents and educating the public.

The most important aspects of public institutions' activities are:

- creation of legal and regulatory frameworks: Public institutions introduce legislation to protect critical infrastructure, personal data and the digital economy. An example is the Polish Act on the National CS System (ActKSB 2018) (Journal of Laws 2018, item 1560, as amended), which sets out the obligations of critical service operators and digital service providers. The creation of national and sectoral IT security standards allows for a unified approach to data protection and infrastructure, and the implementation of legislation such as GDPR (RODO 2016) aims to ensure the security of citizens' data and protect their privacy;
- monitoring and threat analysis: Incident response centres (e.g. CERT/CSIRT) analyse cyber threat data, carry out monitoring of systems and respond to incidents in real time. Threat warning systems, such as national cyber monitoring platforms, identify attacks before they cause serious damage. The above institutions collect and analyse data on new attack techniques to develop better protection strategies;
- incident response and crisis management: Within state structures, teams are being set up for immediate action in the event of cyberattacks, such as on critical infrastructure. In crisis situations, public institutions play a co-ordinating role between different actors – from the private sector to the uniformed services. Regular simulations of cyberattacks at the national level allow public institutions to prepare for real threats and improve response procedures;
- protection of critical infrastructure: Public institutions identify and classify critical infrastructure, the security of which is crucial to the functioning of the state, such as power grids, water pipelines or transport systems. Laws and regulations require critical infrastructure operators to implement advanced protection mechanisms, and organising audits and penetration tests of critical infrastructure allows vulnerabilities to be detected and eliminated;
- international cooperation: Public institutions participate in the activities of organisations such as NATO, ENISA (European CS Agency) or INTERPOL, supporting global CS initiatives. In addition, they cooperate with foreign partners in the exchange of threat data and best practices. Participation in international cyberattack simulations, such as NATO Locked Shields, allows for the improvement of defence capabilities;
- education and public support: Educational campaigns by public institutions, such as "Safer Internet" or programmes related to data protection, increase citizens' awareness of cyber threats. Institutions,

on the other hand, offer advice and training to businesses, especially small- and medium-sized ones, which often lack the resources to protect themselves against cyber threats by organising courses and postgraduate studies for CS professionals to ensure access to highly qualified personnel.

- development of security infrastructure and technology: Public institutions support the development of technologies such as quantum encryption, BD analytics or AI systems that can significantly improve security. In addition, they support the construction and development of national CS centres and state-level threat monitoring systems. The state, in return, offers financial support to companies and research institutions developing security technologies, which significantly improves CS;
- cooperation with the private sector: Public–private partnerships, that is, the creation of joint initiatives that allow for a better understanding of threats and the development of effective protection strategies. Public institutions additionally provide the private sector with information on new threats, security gaps and possible ways to address them. Knowledge-sharing forums, conferences, workshops and webinars are often organised, where the public and private sectors can share experiences and ideas.

In summary, public institutions act as a pillar of CS, providing consistent regulation, oversight of infrastructure and co-ordination in the event of incidents. Their effectiveness depends on cooperation with the private sector, advanced technologies and involvement in international initiatives. In an era of rapid technological development, adequate state support and action are crucial to protect citizens and the economy from the growing threats in cyberspace.

Today's world, based on rapidly evolving technologies, presents society with new CS challenges. The increasing digitalisation of everyday life, the development of AI, the IoT and cloud infrastructure and the global dependence on technology create both enormous opportunities and significant risks. CS has become not only a technical but also a strategic issue of critical importance to national security, the economy and individual privacy. In summary, CS in an era of rapid technological development requires a comprehensive approach that combines advanced technologies, effective international cooperation, consistent regulation and public education. Concerted action and innovative approaches are necessary to effectively counter threats and ensure stability and security in an increasingly digitalised world. The future of CS depends on the ability to adapt quickly to new technologies and challenges, making both countries and their citizens better prepared to deal with constantly evolving threats.

1.4 TECHNOLOGICAL THREATS TO INTERNAL AND EXTERNAL SECURITY

Technological threats to internal and external security can be categorised into several main categories that arise from the dynamic development of technology and its impact on various aspects of states and societies. Much of it has been discussed previously, so here the focus is on reviewing and discussing those that have not yet been written about. Key threats include:

- cybercrime and cyberattacks such as attacks on critical infrastructure (e.g. power plants, water supply systems and public transport), ransomware, DDoS attacks, data theft, disinformation and information manipulation;
- AI and automation, deepfake, AI in cyberattacks (automatic detection of security vulnerabilities by malicious algorithms), weapons automation (development of autonomous warfare systems that can operate without human intervention, e.g. the STM Kargu-2 (Гойденко & Рожнов 2022), Jaeger-C (Kleczkowska 2023) or US Air Force MQ-9 Reaper (Sirota 2021)) and algorithmic threat;
- IoT, lack of security features in IoT devices, allowing attacks on smart homes, cars or cities, and mass data collection by devices that can be used to invade privacy;
- cyber weapons and hybrid warfare. Contemporary conflicts are increasingly moving beyond the traditional battlefield to include cyberspace and operations in the information sphere. Cyber weapons and hybrid warfare are key challenges to both the internal and external security of states. Cyber weapons (Jacobsen 2021) are tools or techniques used to launch attacks in cyberspace. They can be used by states, criminal groups or even individuals to achieve strategic, military or economic objectives. Types of cyber weapons include malware, viruses, worms, Trojan horses, ransomware, zero-day attacks, DDoS attacks and electronic weapons (disruption of radio communications, GPS systems and other technology-dependent infrastructure). Cyber weapons are used to attack critical infrastructure (blackouts caused by attacks on power grids, e.g. Ukraine, 2015–2016), industrial sabotage (Stuxnet), cyber espionage and disruption of military operations (use of cyberattacks to disrupt the chain of command and communication systems). Hybrid warfare (Kamionka 2023) combines traditional methods of warfare with irregular

and technological operations such as cyberattacks and information warfare. The aim is to weaken the adversary without direct military confrontation. Hybrid warfare is characterised by asymmetric actions, that is, exploiting the opponent's weaknesses in specific areas, such as Russian actions in Ukraine after the annexation of Crimea in 2014. Lacking a clear front line, attacks are carried out in cyberspace, in the media and by paramilitary groups. Disruption of political and social processes is through disinformation, propaganda and manipulation of public opinion. Local social conflicts, inspiring or supporting separatist movements or rebel groups, are often used. Tools of hybrid warfare include cyberattacks (paralysing administrative, banking and military systems), information warfare (spreading fake news to destabilise society), support for irregular armed forces (funding or arming local groups), economic pressure (sanctions and manipulation of commodity prices) and intelligence operations (collecting data and using it to blackmail or destabilise an opponent's operations). Examples of hybrid warfare include Russia's actions in Ukraine (annexation of Crimea in 2014, through the actions of "green men" and cyberattacks, various disinformation campaigns against the Ukrainian authorities), in China (expansion in Southeast Asia using economic pressure and cyberattacks) and ISIS attacks (use of the Internet for propaganda, recruitment and co-ordination of terrorist attacks). Effects of the use of cyber weapons and hybrid warfare: Political (destabilisation of governments, undermining their authority), economic (financial losses resulting from cyberattacks on the banking or industrial sector), social (increased distrust of state institutions and polarisation of society) and military (weakening of state defence capabilities). Countering the use of cyber weapons and hybrid warfare and defence in terms of CS is investing in modern protection technologies and creating rapid response teams for cyber threats (e.g. CERT). In terms of international cooperation, it is the exchange of threat information and joint exercises. In terms of public education, it is raising awareness of disinformation and cyber threats. And in terms of regulation, it is the creation of laws adapted to new types of conflict. In terms of detection and response, it is the development of AI systems to detect hostile actions in cyberspace. In summary, cyber weapons and hybrid warfare are increasingly common in global conflicts. They require states to take a multidimensional approach to defence that combines technology, policy, education and international cooperation. It is also crucial to respond quickly to new threats that emerge in a rapidly changing technological environment;

- biotechnology and genetic technology: The dynamic development of biotechnology and genetic technology carries enormous potential to improve life, including in medicine, agriculture or environmental protection. At the same time, these same technologies pose serious threats to the internal and external security of states. Bioterrorism (Mrożek 2023) enables the creation of biological weapons that can be used by terrorist groups, criminals or hostile states. Features of bioterrorism include the creation of new pathogens (CRISPR technology (Cheng et al. 2022) allows gene editing and modification of existing microorganisms to increase their virulence, resistance to treatment or transmissibility), the ability to mass produce (the development of bioreactors allows rapid multiplication of pathogens) and the difficulty of detection (biological agents can be difficult to detect before they are used, increasing their effectiveness as a tool of terror). Examples of possible bioterrorist applications include the spread of modified viruses (viruses, such as influenza or coronaviruses, can be genetically modified to increase their ability to infect humans), attacks on food infrastructure (introduction of pathogens that destroy crops or animal farms, leading to famine) and targeted introduction of immune diseases (design of pathogens that target specific populations). Biohacking (Meyer 2020) is the modification of the genes of organisms, including humans, outside official scientific institutions. This phenomenon is gaining popularity due to the availability of gene-editing technology. Threats arising from biohacking include amateur gene editing (individuals without proper training can create dangerous microorganisms), modification of the human genome (attempts to create "enhanced" humans, e.g. increasing their physical fitness or intelligence, can lead to unpredictable health and ethical consequences) and the possibility of deliberate action (biohackers can deliberately create biohazards, e.g. for blackmail purposes). Biological weapons (Chrzanowska & Plewa 2023) are the use of microorganisms, toxins or biological agents to cause damage to human, animal or environmental populations. Types of biological weapons: Weapons based on viruses and bacteria (anthrax, smallpox and Ebola virus), biological agents of mass destruction (pathogens capable of rapid transmission and causing mass deaths) and biological toxins (substances such as botulism or ricin can be used to deliberately poison people). Features of biological weapons: Difficulty in controlling proliferation (biological weapons can spread beyond their intended target population), low cost of production (compared to other weapons, biological agents can be relatively cheap to produce) and destabilising potential (fear and panic caused by a biological attack can lead to social chaos). Genetic manipulation for military purposes (Fatollahi Arani & Zeinoddini 2023): Genetic technology can be used to deliberately design organisms to serve as weapons in international conflicts. Examples of such applications include designing pathogens that target specific ethnic groups (using population genetics to create bioweapons that target specific genotypes), modifying organisms for sabotage (introducing invasive species into enemy ecosystems to destabilise the environment) and stimulating pandemics (large-scale dissemination of artificially created pathogens). The cloning of organisms (Jasudowicz 2001), including humans, poses a number of ethical and security challenges. Threats posed by cloning include cloning humans for military purposes (creating soldiers with optimised physical or mental characteristics), human experimentation (cloning attempts may lead to inhumane experiments, violating human rights) and threats to biodiversity (mass cloning may reduce the genetic diversity of species). Biodiversity threats (Prakash & Verma 2022): Modern genetic technologies, such as GMOs (Rezaei et al. 2023), can affect ecosystems in ways that are difficult to predict. Examples of such risks include accidental release of modified organisms (GMOs can disrupt the balance of ecosystems that have been established for years), creation of superweeds (crossing GMO plants with wild species can lead to herbicide-resistant weeds) and genetic depletion (dominance of GMO plants or animals can lead to a reduction in genetic diversity). Addressing the threats posed by the development of biotechnology involves regulation (international treaties such as the Convention on the Prohibition of the Development, Production and Stockpiling of Bacteriological (Biological) and Toxin Weapons and on Their Destruction – BWC) (Convention 1972), technology monitoring (establishment of global monitoring systems for biotechnology and genetic research), international cooperation (cooperation in information sharing and response to biological threats) and public education (raising awareness of the risks and responsible use of genetic technologies). In summary, biotechnology and genetic technology represent both a huge opportunity and a serious threat. They can be used not only to protect health, increase food production or protect the environment but also for the deliberate creation of biological weapons, bioterrorism or genetic manipulation with unpredictable consequences. It is crucial to develop regulatory, monitoring and international cooperation mechanisms to minimise the risks associated with their misuse;

- quantum technologies, which include QC (Ladd et al. 2010), quantum cryptography (Gisin et al. 2002) and quantum communication systems (Hasan et al. 2023), represent one of the most promising yet dangerous areas of modern technology. Their development not only has the potential to revolutionise many fields but also carries significant threats to the internal and external security of states. QCs are devices that use the principles of quantum mechanics, such as superposition and entanglement, to perform calculations that are much faster than traditional computers. However, they generate certain risks. Threats to current cryptographic systems: Breaking asymmetric cryptography (algorithms (Górniak & Kopniak 2017) such as RSA, ECC or DSA, which are the basis for the security of many systems) can be broken by QC using the Shor algorithm (Ugwuishiwu et al. 2020). This means that data protected by current methods can be decrypted), the breaking of security protocols in communications (data sent over the Internet, e.g. financial transactions and government communications, can become vulnerable to interception and decryption) and the loss of historical information secrecy (if data is currently stored in encrypted form, it could be decrypted in the future by a QC, posing a threat to government archives and military secrets). Potential consequences of the development of QC include the destabilisation of financial systems, the compromise of state and intelligence secrets and the possibility of manipulating critical infrastructure (e.g. power or transport networks). Quantum cryptography, based on principles of quantum mechanics such as quantum entanglement and Heisenberg's indeterminacy principle, promises near-perfect security in communications. On the other hand, it carries certain risks. Threats associated with quantum cryptography include the technology race (countries and organisations seeking a technological advantage may invest huge resources in developing quantum cryptography, which can lead to CS inequalities), military applications (quantum cryptography can provide non-transitory communication channels that can be exploited in military operations or by terrorist groups) and critical data sharing (countries with advanced quantum cryptography can effectively protect their data, leaving other countries vulnerable to attacks). Quantum communication networks (systems), such as quantum teleportation and quantum entanglement systems, can be used to transmit information quickly and securely. The risks associated with quantum communication systems are the exclusivity of the technology (countries with advanced quantum communication systems can gain a strategic advantage, leaving other countries behind), the possibility of interception and control (although quantum communication systems are theoretically resistant to eavesdropping, there are still risks associated with technical limitations and implementation errors) and the disruption of quantum communication channels (attacks involving the introduction of quantum noise can disrupt communication systems). The development of quantum technologies not only has great potential in the military sector but also carries the risk of destabilising global security. Examples of risks include quantum radar systems (Torromé & Barzanjeh 2024) (enables detection of stealth objects (Kitahara et al. 2004) (e.g. aircraft) with unprecedented accuracy), quantum navigation systems (Feng 2019) (enables navigation without the need for GPS satellites, making it difficult to disrupt these systems) and quantum simulation (Daley et al. 2022) (advanced simulation of nuclear and chemical processes could accelerate the development of weapons of mass destruction). Economic and social impacts of quantum technologies: The development of quantum technology could lead to significant changes in the global economy that could affect political and social stability. Threats include a technology race (countries investing in quantum technology may dominate key economic sectors such as finance, trade and technology), technological inequality (a lack of access to quantum technologies by developing countries may lead to a further widening of the economic gap) and disruption of labour markets (the replacement of traditional systems by quantum technologies may lead to the obsolescence of many professions). Addressing the risks of quantum technologies: Steps at the international level are the introduction of international treaty regulation (development of international standards for the use of quantum technologies, similar to nuclear weapons), international cooperation (creation of scientific and technological consortia to support the development of responsible use of quantum technologies) and monitoring of the technology race (international organisations should monitor the development of quantum technologies to prevent monopolisation of the technology). In terms of national initiatives, these include investment in research and development (countries should invest in developing their own quantum technology capabilities to avoid technological dependence), training of professionals (educating new generations of scientists and engineers capable of working in the field of quantum technologies) and the implementation of post-quantum cryptography (Bernstein & Lange 2017) (preparing information systems for the advent of QC by introducing algorithms that are resistant to them). In summary, quantum technologies have the potential to revolutionise many aspects of life, but their misuse can lead to serious threats to global security. It is crucial that states and international organisations work towards the responsible development and implementation of these technologies, while investing in protective mechanisms against potential threats;

- autonomous vehicles and drones are among the fastest-growing technologies in robotics and AI. While they have many positive applications, such as deliveries, public transport or rescue operations, their use in the wrong way can lead to serious threats to internal and external security. Autonomous vehicles, such as cars or trucks, can become a target or tool in criminal and terrorist activities. Threats associated with autonomous vehicles include cyberattacks related to vehicle takeover. Autonomous control systems are vulnerable to hacking attacks, which can lead to deliberately causing road accidents or using vehicles as tools of attack. Manipulation of navigation systems: Attacks on GPS systems can alter a vehicle's route, leading to chaos in logistics or threats to passengers. Use in terrorist attacks: Trap cars can be programmed to carry explosives and detonate them at a specific place and time. Remote attacks: Autonomous vehicles can be used to ram crowds, buildings or critical infrastructure without the need for a driver. Disruption of transport infrastructure: Attacks on a fleet of autonomous vehicles can cause chaos in public and private transport. Threats: Real-world tests have shown that autonomous vehicle systems can be fooled by modifications to road signs, which can be exploited by criminals, and hacking experiments have shown that vehicles can be remotely stopped or accelerated, which significantly affects safety. Drones, both commercial and military, are increasingly used in civilian and military operations. Their wide availability means that they are being used not only for positive purposes but also for criminal and terrorist activities. Drone threats include terrorist and criminal attacks (carrying explosives, attacks on public figures, disruption of airports, espionage and data theft, theft of intellectual property, disruption of public order and military offensive applications from swarming drone systems to asymmetric threats). Threat countermeasures are technological actions (drone defence systems, CS of autonomous vehicles or geofencing). Legal actions: Regulation of drones and autonomous vehicles, control of sales and access to the technology, and penalties for abuse. In the field of international action, international cooperation (countries should cooperate in monitoring and preventing the illegal use of drones and autonomous vehicles) and the development of technological standards are required. In summary, autonomous vehicles and drones are both an opportunity and a threat. They can significantly improve efficiency in many sectors,

> but their misuse risks destabilising security at the local, national and international levels. It is crucial to develop appropriate regulations, develop protective technologies and strengthen international cooperation to minimise the risks associated with their use.

Technological threats to internal and external security require appropriate countermeasures to minimise their impact and protect society and infrastructure. One key element of prevention is the development of advanced protection technologies. In the area of CS, it is necessary to develop a more resilient digital infrastructure, including the implementation of systems based on post-quantum cryptography, which will protect data from potential threats associated with the development of QC. Protecting information systems also requires the implementation of advanced tools to detect and neutralise cyberattacks, such as AI to analyse network traffic patterns and identify suspicious activity in real time. At the same time, investment should be made in the development of anti-drone technology, including electromagnetic and laser defence systems, which can effectively neutralise the threat of drones being used in criminal or terrorist activities. Geofencing, or the designation of no-fly zones, should be integrated with airspace management systems to prevent incidents in sensitive areas such as airports, military bases or power plants. It is also crucial to increase scrutiny of the sale of advanced technologies, such as autonomous vehicles and drones, in order to prevent their acquisition by actors who may use them in harmful ways. Education and training are equally important in the context of countering technological threats. The public and national security personnel should be aware of the risks associated with new technologies and know the methods to neutralise them. Training in CS, recognition of threats from autonomous systems or procedures for responding to technological attacks should become an integral part of training programmes in the uniformed services and the public sector. In addition to national efforts, international cooperation in addressing technological threats is also necessary. Countries should create common strategies and regulations for the safe use of advanced technologies and exchange information on new forms of threats. Creating global technology standards, such as those for autonomous vehicles, drones or quantum systems, will reduce the risk of misuse. Cooperation among governments, international organisations and the private sector is key to effectively monitoring and countering threats. Ultimately, it is important that technological development is carried out in a responsible and sustainable manner. Regulations should take into account both the potential benefits of advanced technologies and the risks that may arise from their misuse. Investing in research into protective technologies, developing the security infrastructure and building public awareness will reduce risks and prepare states and societies for the challenges of the technological changes of the future.

NOTES

1 An application programming interface (API) is an interface that allows communication between different applications or systems. It allows access to software functions and data without having to know its internal structure. Examples are REST API, GraphQL or WebSocket own development.

2 A pipeline (in the context of AI) is an automated sequence of processes which encompasses all stages of working with AI data and models in-house development.

Social and cultural aspects of AI

2

AI is having a significant impact on society and culture, changing many aspects of everyday life. The automation of work is leading to transformations in the employment market, not only replacing some professions but also creating new opportunities for highly skilled professionals. Increasing human interaction with AI, such as chatbots or voice assistants, is impacting the way people communicate and relate to each other, sometimes leading to loneliness. AI algorithms can reinforce existing social biases, raising questions about accountability for their decisions in areas such as medicine or justice. AI is also changing perceptions of creativity, as algorithms are able to create music, paintings or literature, raising questions about the role of humans in the arts. Cultural differences affect the way AI is developed and used, for example, in privacy or efficiency priorities. Language models often marginalise smaller cultural groups, which can lead to a loss of diversity. Building public trust in AI technologies through transparency and appropriate regulation is key. AI has the potential to support cultural diversity, for example, by protecting minority languages and promoting local traditions. Education and raising public awareness of the opportunities and risks of AI are essential if society is to take an active role in shaping the future of this technology.

2.1 PERCEPTIONS OF AI IN DIFFERENT CULTURES AND RELIGIONS

Perceptions of AI in different cultures and religions depend on the specific characteristics of the community, its values, beliefs and level of technological advancement. AI is perceived differently depending on the culture, history and

DOI: 10.1201/9781003644194-3

social context, which are specific to each continent. These differences affect how AI is adapted, developed and regulated in each region. In North America, AI perceived as a new technology is becoming an engine of progress. In the United States (Kelley et al. 2021) and Canada, AI is seen primarily as a tool for innovation and an engine for the digital economy. The dominant narrative associated with AI focuses on the potential for industrial development, competitive advantage and technological dominance. Hollywood has played a significant role in shaping the perception of AI as both a promising and potentially dangerous technology. Films such as Terminator, Matrix and Her explore various aspects of the coexistence of humans and machines. In the United States, there is a particular focus on privacy regulation, social inequality and the potential dangers of workplace automation. The Canadian approach to AI is more humane, with an emphasis on human rights and the development of technologies for the public good. In Europe, AI is seen as a tool to support societal values in the context of values such as equality, human rights and privacy. The European Union plays a key role in shaping regulations that aim at the ethical use of AI. Many European countries are focusing on the creation of "trusted AI" (Ma et al. 2023) to comply with the principles of transparency and accountability. Europeans are more sceptical about AI than people on other continents, which may be due to a history of technological conflicts (e.g. fear of surveillance in former Eastern Bloc countries). Scandinavian countries see AI as a tool to improve the quality of life and protect the environment, while Central and Eastern Europe often see AI as an opportunity to catch up with the more technologically developed countries of the West. In Asia, especially in countries such as Japan, South Korea and China, AI is seen very positively as a key part of the technological and social future. These countries are investing huge resources in the development of AI, seeing it as a tool for global technological dominance. In Japan, this is influenced by traditional Shintoist beliefs, which attribute spirituality even to inanimate objects. Therefore, robots and AI are accepted as "beings" (Bukowski & Klonowska 2024) that can cooperate with humans. In China, AI is part of a larger state strategy. The government is promoting its development in education, industry and government, although there are concerns about surveillance and social control. India is betting on AI as a tool for economic development, with a focus on agriculture, medicine and education. In Southeast Asia, AI is more associated with access to technologies that can improve the quality of life. In Africa, AI is seen in many African countries as an opportunity to address issues such as poverty and inadequate access to education or healthcare. Investments in AI are focused on practical applications such as agriculture (e.g. crop monitoring) or financial services (e.g. microfinance systems). The main problem in adapting AI in Africa is the lack of infrastructure, digital exclusion and limited human resources to handle modern technologies. There are also concerns that AI may increase inequalities between developed and developing countries. In South America, AI is seen as a tool to improve key sectors such as public safety, education and healthcare. AI is also being used in the fight against crime, for example, to analyse data in police systems. The big challenge in developing AI technology in South America is the lack of funding and infrastructure. Public concerns include the potential for increased political control and reduced citizen privacy. In Australia and Oceania (New Zealand), AI is seen as a tool for the development of the agricultural sector, environmental protection and public services. Protection against climate risks is of great importance, and AI is used to monitor environmental change. The region places a strong emphasis on the ethical use of AI, particularly in the context of protecting the rights of indigenous peoples such as Aborigines and Māori. In summary, cultural differences in perceptions of AI stem from local conditions such as traditions, beliefs, economic development and access to technology. In some regions, AI is seen as a partner and a tool for improving quality of life, while in others, it raises concerns about ethics, social control and inequality. These differences are crucial for global cooperation in the development and regulation of AI.

Perceptions of AI in different cultures and communities are deeply rooted in belief systems and religious and spiritual traditions. Religions and local beliefs play a key role in shaping opinions on the ethics, potential and limitations of AI (Lane 2021).

Christianity, especially in its mainline denominations (Catholicism, Protestantism and Orthodoxy), views AI as a human creation that has no soul or capacity for spiritual experience. AI is seen as a tool that should be used according to moral principles. Christians emphasise the need to preserve human dignity and control the development of AI so that it does not lead to the dehumanisation of society. Theological questions arise, such as whether AI could be capable of "sin" or whether the moral decisions made by AI are in accordance with divine laws. In Europe, AI is analysed in the context of human rights and Christian values, while in North America, there is often debate about the potential threat AI could pose to freedom and privacy. In Islam, AI is accepted as a human creation, but its development and use must comply with Shariah principles. AI cannot be treated as an equivalent being to a human being because it does not have a soul (*ruh*). Islam places an obligation on the development of AI to serve the common good, provided that the technology does not violate moral and spiritual values. AI used for surveillance or manipulation purposes is criticised, especially in the context of justice and human rights. In the Gulf countries, AI is seen as a tool for economic development, but there is concern that too much machine autonomy may violate faith principles. In Buddhism, AI can be seen as a neutral tool that, like other technologies, can be used to do good or evil, depending on the intention of the user. Buddhists do not grant AI the ability to achieve enlightenment because it lacks consciousness and the capacity to suffer. The development of AI should follow the principles of compassion (*karuna*) and wisdom (*prajna*). It can be used to reduce suffering, such as in medicine or education. In Buddhist countries such as Japan and South Korea, AI is seen more as a tool for harmonious cooperation with people. Hinduism, based on concepts of spirituality and reincarnation, sees AI as a creation devoid of atman (soul). AI cannot participate in the cycle of life and death and is therefore incapable of spiritual development. In Hinduism, there are philosophical questions as to whether AI can be seen as a kind of "life" from a technological, though not spiritual, perspective. There is an acceptance of AI as a tool to improve the quality of life, especially in areas such as medicine or education.

India, as one of the leading countries developing AI, sees the technology as a way to improve the socio-economic situation, but with a spiritual heritage. In Judaism, AI is treated as a creation of man, which has no soul or spiritual capacity. Judaism emphasises the responsibility of humans to create and control AI. AI must be compatible with ethical values such as justice (*tzedek*) and the protection of life (*pikuach nefesh*). In the Jewish tradition, AI can raise questions about the boundary between human creativity and divine power over the world. In Israel, AI is used in advanced defence and medical technologies, raising ethical questions about its use in conflict. In Shintoism, which is the dominant belief system in Japan, all objects, even inanimate objects, can have spirits (kami). This promotes the acceptance of AI and robots as "living" collaborators with humans. The Shintoist approach to spirituality facilitates the integration of AI and robots into society. Examples such as robot assistants in elderly care are seen as a natural extension of technology. AI should coexist with humans in harmony, reflecting the Japanese culture of balance and community. In many traditional African beliefs, technology is seen as something that must interact with nature and spirituality. AI can be accepted if its use benefits the community. AI is seen as a tool to solve problems such as lack of access to education, drinking water or healthcare, but with respect for local values. There are concerns that AI may violate the traditional spiritual order, especially if it is seen as too autonomous. Atheism and secularism: In societies with a more secular world-view (e.g. in Northern Europe), AI is mainly treated as a technological tool, without spiritual connotations. Atheist societies often focus on the pragmatic aspects of AI development, such as regulation, privacy and human rights. AI is seen as a key element of the technological future but is subject to careful ethical and social analyses. In summary, religions and beliefs shape diverse perspectives on AI. In many spiritual traditions, AI is treated as a human-made tool that should be used ethically and in accordance with local values. These differences highlight the need for a global intercultural dialogue so that AI is developed in a way that is responsible and respectful of the diversity of beliefs and cultures.

2.2 GENERATIONAL DIFFERENCES IN RELATION TO NEW TECHNOLOGIES

Generational differences towards new technologies are due to different experiences, upbringing and speed of adaptation to technological change. The Baby Boomer generation (Hughes & Angela 2004) (born before 1965) grew up at a time when technologies were limited to simple devices such as a radio or television. They often see modern technologies as tools to be "mastered" and understood, which involves some effort and sometimes fear of using them. Their approach tends to be cautious – they want to be sure that a new tool is safe and useful before they decide to use it. Many people of this generation prefer to use tried and tested solutions, which can lead to difficulties in adapting to new systems, such as switching to banking apps or digital communications. Even simple devices such as smartphones can be a challenge for them if they lack an intuitive introduction. The main motivation for learning is need. They use technology when necessary (e.g. at work and to contact family). They often learn through traditional instruction (paper tutorials or support from relatives). Generation X (Kupperschmidt 1998) (born between 1965 and 1980) were brought up during the dynamic introduction of personal computers, which allowed them to come into contact with technology at an early stage of its development. They see technology mainly as a tool for work, productivity and organisation of daily life. They are more open to new technologies than Baby Boomers but less fascinated by them than younger generations. They often use technology in a pragmatic way, for example, to manage finances, communicate professionally or organise family responsibilities. They are eager to learn new technologies if they see practical value in them, but they are sometimes critical of trends that they consider "unnecessary" or overly complicated. Generation Y (Eisner 2005) (Millennials, born between 1981 and 1996) grew up with the rise of the Internet and mobile phones, making technology a natural part of life for them. They see technology as a tool for both work and entertainment, as well as a way to build social relationships. They are open-minded and curious about new things, often adapting quickly to new trends such as mobile apps, social media and streaming platforms. They use technology not only to facilitate daily activities but also to build their identity (e.g. through social media activity). They learn intuitively, often by trial and error. They are motivated not only by need but also by the desire to be "up to date" with the latest technological trends. Generation Z (Dolot 2018) (born after 1996) are the so-called digital natives who have had access to the Internet, smartphones and other modern technologies since childhood. Technology is not a tool for them but a natural environment. They often do not see it as "something new" but as an integral part of life. They pick up new tools and applications quickly, rarely feeling the need to read instructions. Very open to innovations, especially those related to social interaction (social media and streaming platforms) and entertainment (video games and VR). Motivation to learn is linked to the desire to explore and experiment. In summary, older generations (Baby Boomers and part of Generation X) treat technology mainly as a practical tool that takes time and commitment to master. Younger generations (Millennials and Gen Z) are more flexible, seeing technology as an integral part of life, a tool for self-expression and a way to build social relationships. A key difference is how they adapt. Older generations require support and time, while younger generations assimilate novelties almost intuitively. Technology is also a means of self-expression for them, for example, by creating video content, graphics or music using apps and programmes.

If we consider the way we use technology when it comes to communication, the Baby Boomer generation prefers traditional forms of communication, such as phone calls or face-to-face meetings. Email is often their preferred digital form of communication, especially in a professional context. They are less likely to use instant messaging (e.g. WhatsApp and Messenger) and see social media as a way to keep in touch with family and friends. Generation X is keen to use mobile phones, both to talk and to send text messages. Social media is important to them, although they use it mainly to keep in touch professionally (e.g. LinkedIn) or with family (Facebook). They are moderate in their use of instant messaging and apps – preferring tried-and-tested and functional tools. Generation Y prefers instant messaging (Messenger, WhatsApp and Discord) and social media as primary communication channels. They are more likely to use asynchronous communication (messaging and email) than phone calls. They use video applications (e.g. Zoom and Teams) for both work and private life. Generation Z communicates mainly through quick messages (Snapchat, WhatsApp and Instagram Direct) or social media apps. They make phone calls infrequently and instead prefer video calls (FaceTime and Messenger). They often use the audio/video features of apps such as TikTok, YouTube or Discord as a way to interact socially. When it comes to entertainment, the Baby Boomer generation is more likely to choose traditional media such as TV, radio or newspapers. If they use the Internet, it is mainly to read the news, watch YouTube videos or listen to music. Computer games are rare. They more often choose puzzle games (e.g. Sudoku and solitaire). Generation X uses both traditional and digital forms of entertainment. They are keen to watch TV and use streaming platforms (Netflix and Amazon Prime). Computer games are popular, especially those from the 1980s and 1990s, which are reminiscent of their youth. Generation Y prefers digital entertainment: Streaming platforms, computer games and sites such as YouTube. They eagerly participate in online multiplayer games (e.g. Fortnite and League of Legends). Social media is an important part of entertainment (memes, videos and podcasts). For Generation Z, entertainment is interactive and multichannel: Video games, streaming (e.g. Twitch) and social media apps (TikTok, Instagram). They often combine different activities: Watching Twitch broadcasts while playing games or listening to podcasts. Short-form videos and content created by other users are very popular for Generation Z. In terms of education and knowledge acquisition, the Baby Boomer generation prefers traditional learning methods such as books, printed materials and live lectures. They face difficulties in digital education, especially in using e-learning platforms or educational apps. Searching for information on the Internet (e.g. Google and Wikipedia) is often their main technological support tool. Generation X combines traditional learning methods with modern tools such as webinars or e-learning. It uses search engines and learning platforms (Coursera and Udemy) for self-learning, is open to using technology for work and learning but often chooses tried-and-tested sources. For Generation Y, technology is an integral part of their education. Generation Y uses online courses, mobile apps, instructional videos and podcasts, eagerly uses social media to learn and share knowledge, values flexibility in learning and uses mobile devices to learn anywhere, anytime. Generation Z learns mainly in a digital environment through the use of educational apps, online courses and video tutorials on YouTube and often learns on the fly by searching for quick answers to questions on Google or TikTok (e.g. short educational videos). It is used for remote education and the use of tools such as Zoom or Google Classroom. In terms of shopping and use of services, the Baby Boomer generation, prefer traditional shopping in stationary shops, although they increasingly use online shopping, especially on large platforms (e.g. Allegro and Amazon). They are often wary of online payments and are more likely to use cash-on-delivery options. Generation X uses both traditional and digital shopping methods, values the security and convenience of online shopping but may be sceptical of new platforms or mobile apps. For Generation Y, online shopping is standard, and mobile apps (e.g. Allegro, Zalando and Amazon) are very popular. They are eager to take advantage of promotions and loyalty programmes available online and often use online reviews and social media to make purchasing decisions. Generation Z uses online shopping most often, from e-commerce platforms to social media (shopping on Instagram or TikTok), uses modern payment methods such as BLIK, PayPal or Apple Pay and is open to new trends, such as purchasing products in AR. In terms of social relationships and interactions, older generations build relationships mainly in the real world and treat technology as a tool to foster contact, while younger generations often develop relationships online. Social media, video games and forums are the places where they meet and interact.

Adaptation to new technologies varies from generation to generation and is based on their previous experiences, comfort level with technology and openness to change. Baby Boomers are often wary of new technologies, especially if their introduction requires a change in habits. They fear mistakes and improper use. For this generation, adopting new things requires more detailed instructions, as intuitive use of technology can be difficult. They often rely on help from younger family members or training to understand new devices or applications. Over time, they adapt to technologies such as smartphones or social media but use them mainly for basic activities (calls, photos and contact with family). They may reject novelties that seem too complicated, such as financial management apps or advanced smartphone features. They feel fear of data loss or online security, such as online fraud. They need more repetition and time to master new technologies. Generation X mainly adopt new technologies when they see their practical benefits in their professional or everyday lives. They are open to novelty but often combine it with existing solutions, such as using desktop computers alongside smartphones. Their youth was during the computer revolution, so many have developed the ability to adapt to technology later in life. They are willing to use platforms such as e-learning or online banking if they see the convenience and benefits. They are less likely to use technology purely for entertainment than younger generations. They are not always up to date with the latest technology trends, which may make them feel less confident interacting with younger users. Millennials grew up in a time of rapid Internet development, which makes them accustomed to frequent technological changes. They are inclined to discover the functions of new devices or applications on their own, rarely using manuals. They integrate technology into both their professional and private lives, for example, using apps to manage their time, health or finances. They adapt quickly to new trends such as social media, mobile apps or streaming services. They are eager to share their experiences with new technologies online, for example, by reviewing products or publishing tutorials. Sometimes, they embrace technology uncritically, which can lead to over-reliance on it and ignoring potential risks, such as privacy. Generation Z grew up in the technology age, so adaptation to newness is almost automatic for them. They often adopt new tools without the need for instruction, relying on intuition and exploration. New applications, devices or platforms are assimilated instantly, and their use becomes natural in everyday life. They are eager to experiment with the latest technologies such as AR, AI or content creation apps (TikTok and Canva). They use multiple devices simultaneously (e.g. smartphone, laptop and smartwatch) and switch seamlessly between them. They tend to abandon technologies that do not offer immediate benefits or satisfaction. They present a lack of in-depth understanding of how technology works, while they are willing to use off-the-shelf solutions but are less interested in their technical underpinnings. If we compare the speed of adaptation, Baby Boomers represents the slowest adaptation process, due to technological barriers and less openness to change;

Generation X represents moderate speed of adaptation and is open to novelty but guided by practicality when making choices; Millennials represent fast adaptation due to skills acquired in times of rapid technological development; and Generation Z represents the fastest adaptation, as they grew up in an environment full of technology and are used to frequent change. In terms of barriers and motivations for adaptation, for Baby Boomers, barriers are fear of the unknown and inexperience, and motivations are facilitation of daily life and contact with family; for Generation X, the barrier is the lack of time to learn new technologies, and motivations are convenience and efficiency in work and personal life; for Millennials, the barrier is possibility of novelty overload, and motivations are trends, innovation and optimisation of daily activities; and for Generation Z, the barrier is the lack of patience with technologies requiring a longer adaptation process, and motivations are exploration, entertainment and self-expression.

The development of technology has also introduced dynamic changes in the way society functions, which affect different generations differently. As a result, intergenerational challenges have emerged due to different experiences, approaches to technology and adaptability. Differences in the rate of technological adaptation: Younger generations (Millennials and Generation Z) are quick to adopt new technologies and implement them immediately in their daily lives. They are often the first users of new apps, platforms or devices. Older generations (Baby Boomers and Generation X) need more time to understand and learn how to use new tools. They may also be more wary of change. The challenge is that younger generations may feel frustration towards elders, whom they perceive as "slower" to adapt. In turn, elders may feel technologically excluded or overwhelmed by the pace of change. Differences in attitudes to privacy and security: Younger generations often use technology without much concern for security. They share a lot of information on social media, sometimes completely unaware of the consequences. Older generations are more sceptical about sharing data online and are concerned about risks such as identity theft and online fraud. The intergenerational challenge is that younger generations may perceive older generations as "overly cautious", while older generations perceive younger generations as "reckless" when it comes to security. Differences in modes of communication: Younger generations prefer quick forms of communication, such as text messaging, instant messaging or social media. Older generations prefer phone calls or face-to-face meetings, considering them more personal. The challenge is the conflicts that can arise when older generations expect a more traditional form of communication and younger generations prefer fast, digital interactions. The gap in technological skills: Younger generations have grown up in the digital age and use modern technology naturally. They have an intuitive approach to learning the new tools on offer. Older generations need additional training to master technology, and their digital skills may be limited to basic functionality, for example. A challenge may be that employers and families may experience difficulties in transferring technological knowledge to older people, leading to frustration on both sides. Conflicts in the work environment: Younger workers are eager to adopt new tools and technologies, such as team messaging, cloud-based project management systems or process automation. Older generations may prefer traditional working methods such as email communication or paper documentation. Differences in attitudes towards technology can lead to tensions within the team, where older generations may feel pressured and younger generations frustrated at having to adapt to older ways of working. Perception of the value of technology: Older generations may see technology as a tool for specific purposes, such as work or communication. Younger generations see technology as an integral part of their lives, using it for entertainment, education, relationships and self-expression. However, older generations may criticise younger generations for being "addicted" to technology, while younger generations may see older generations as "not understanding" the modern world. Intergenerational education: Younger generations often act as teachers in families, helping older members to master new technologies. Older generations may feel uncomfortable asking for help, especially if they encounter frustration or lack of patience from younger generations. The process of technology education between generations requires patience and mutual understanding to avoid tensions and conflicts. The phenomenon of digital exclusion: Older generations are more likely to be digitally excluded because they may not have the skills or resources needed to use new technologies. Younger generations are often unaware of this exclusion and expect everyone to use technology in a similar way to them. The digital divide can lead to the social isolation of older people and limit their access to information or services. Different approaches to work and productivity: Younger generations use technology to automate tasks, work remotely and manage time. Older generations prefer a more traditional approach to work, where technology is an add-on rather than the main tool. There can be confusion in organisations where expectations of efficiency and ways of working differ between generations.

The development of technology has created both a divide and the potential for collaboration between different generations. Building intergenerational bridges in this context requires conscious action at the social, educational and technological levels. Technology education – mutual learning: Older generations need support in learning to use technology, including digital tools, mobile applications or online platforms. Younger generations have a natural ability to absorb technological novelties but can benefit from the experience of elders in terms of ethics, technology history or critical thinking. Bridges' solutions to this problem are intergenerational workshops (organising meetings where younger generations teach older generations how to use technology and older generations share their knowledge and experience), mentoring programmes (creating initiatives where older people teach younger people traditional skills or professional knowledge and younger people help them master digital technologies) and the production of simple educational materials (creating instructions and materials tailored to older users, explaining how technology works in a clear and accessible way). Collaboration in the work environment: Older generations prefer more traditional working methods but bring experience and the ability to think strategically. Younger generations are willing to implement innovative technology solutions that increase efficiency and automate processes. The solution is generationally mixed teams (creating project groups made up of representatives of different generations so as to combine the innovation of the younger with the experience of the older), inclusive training (implementing programmes that teach intergenerational cooperation, with an emphasis on using technology as a tool to facilitate communication and work organisation) and inclusive technology tools (choosing technologies that are intuitive and accessible to all users, regardless of their age). Developing empathy and understanding: Older generations may feel excluded from the digital world or misunderstood by younger generations. Younger generations may assume that older generations "don't want" to use new technologies, rather than recognising their difficulties. The solution is building dialogue (organising intergenerational meetings where participants can share their experiences with technology and explain their needs and concerns), promoting positive role models (showing examples of older people successfully using technology to break stereotypes about their reluctance to innovate) and connecting narratives (creating social or educational campaigns that show how technology can become a bridge between generations). Designing technology that is friendly to all generations: Older generations find it difficult to operate complex interfaces and devices. Younger generations, accustomed to fast, advanced technologies, may not notice that they may be unintuitive for others. The solution is universal design (creating technology adapted to users of different ages, e.g. with larger buttons, simpler messaging language and intuitive navigation), customisation options (allowing users to personalise the interface according to their needs, e.g. changing text size and simplifying menus) and intergenerational testing (involving representatives of different generations in testing new technology products and services). Integration in public and social spaces: Older generations may feel excluded in spaces dominated by new technologies, such as banks that have moved to full automation. Younger generations are often unaware of the difficulties that elders face in accessing such services. The solution is the emergence of digital volunteers (creating programmes in which younger people help older people to use technology in everyday situations, such as online shopping, using banking applications or instant messaging), the creation of technology support sites (organising technology help desks in libraries, community centres or senior centres where older people can receive practical assistance) and the promotion of intergenerational events (organising events that integrate different age groups, such as joint technology workshops or picnics with elements of digital education). Shared technology goals and projects: Older generations can bring knowledge and experience to technology projects. Younger generations bring innovative approaches, energy and technical skills. The solution is hobbies and technology (bringing generations together on projects related to their interests, e.g. creating social media content together, digitally documenting family histories or using travel planning apps) and social projects (working together on initiatives that have a positive impact on the community, e.g. creating digital maps of the neighbourhood or teaching coding to different age groups).

In summary, building technology bridges between generations has numerous benefits that translate into the lives of individuals, society and organisations. Older generations, with the support of younger generations, better understand and use technology in their daily lives, which reduces their sense of exclusion and increases their autonomy. Learning to use new tools, such as mobile apps, instant messaging or online platforms, allows them to participate more actively in social and professional life. By helping older generations master technology, younger generations develop empathy, patience and the ability to adapt to the needs of others. This process strengthens intergenerational relationships and fosters bonds based on mutual support. At the same time, older people, by sharing their knowledge, experience and perspective, can enrich younger people with values that are not always available in the dynamic world of technology. By working together to understand new technologies, the digital divide between generations is reduced, and society as a whole becomes more inclusive and integrated. The inclusion of seniors in the digital world allows them to more easily use e-services, such as health, administration and online shopping platforms. Younger generations, in turn, gain an awareness of the challenges faced by older technology users, which fosters more user-friendly solutions. In the professional context, collaboration between generations benefits organisations by combining the experience and knowledge of older workers with the creativity and technological skills of younger ones. Such integration enhances innovation, efficiency and the ability to solve complex problems. In family relationships, technology can become a bridge that connects generations, enabling closer contact and better understanding. Ultimately, building technology bridges makes society more open and sustainable. Technologies cease to divide people into those who can use them and those who are excluded from this world. Instead, they become a tool for mutual rapprochement that allows us to benefit from generational diversity and build a shared future based on cooperation and mutual respect.

Generational differences towards new technologies are the result of different life experiences, learning styles and habits of accessing innovations. Younger generations, such as Millennials and Generation Z, have grown up in an era of rapid technological development, which makes new tools and solutions a natural part of everyday life for them. They treat technology as an integral aspect of work, learning, entertainment and communication. In contrast, older generations, who began their education and careers in a world without the Internet and mobile devices, often approach novelties with greater reserve or even apprehension. These differences show up in the way they adapt to new technologies – younger people tend to master new devices and applications more quickly, while older people need more time and simpler, more intuitive solutions. This differentiation leads to challenges such as the digital divide or difficulties in intergenerational cooperation at work and in everyday life. At the same time, it creates an opportunity for mutual support – younger people can teach older people how to use new tools, and older people can share their knowledge, experience and critical thinking skills. Understanding these differences is key to building a technology-integrated society where everyone, regardless of age, can benefit from modern solutions. Initiatives such as intergenerational technology workshops, intuitive interface design or programmes supporting digital education for older people help to bridge the generation gap. Through such activities, technology can become a bridge between generations, strengthening family, social and professional relationships, as well as a source of mutual understanding and cooperation. As a result, generational differences need not be an obstacle but can be a force for innovation and social inclusion.

2.3 THE IMPACT OF THE COVID-19 PANDEMIC ON ACCELERATING AI ADAPTATION

The COVID-19 pandemic (Ciotti et al. 2020) has had a significant impact on accelerating AI adaptation in various areas of life and the economy.

Digital transformation in the health sector. AI has been successfully used in the analysis of medical images, such as X-rays and CT scans of the lungs, to diagnose COVID-19 more quickly and accurately. The ML models used have helped to detect characteristic changes in the lungs caused by viral infection, to automate the diagnosis process, significantly easing the burden on medical staff, especially during the peak of the pandemic, and to increase access to diagnosis in regions with limited specialists. AI enabled the creation of epidemiological models that predicted the development of pandemics in time and space. These enabled the identification of areas with the highest risk of new infection outbreaks, the forecasting of resource requirements such as hospital beds, ventilators or vaccines and the planning of preventive actions and the allocation of healthcare resources in real time. AI has also been used in the discovery and testing of new drugs and vaccines. The analysis by NN and AI of large genomic datasets of SARS-CoV-2 has allowed a faster understanding of the structure of the virus. AI algorithms supported the identification of potential therapeutic molecules through computer simulations and reduced the time from laboratory studies to clinical phases through efficient design of experiments. AI enabled significant improvements in remote healthcare. AI-based systems analysed data from devices that monitor patients' conditions at home, such as pulse oximeters and smartwatches. Health chatbots, using NLP, assisted patients with medical information, which relieved the burden on phone lines, and remote medical consultations using AI were used to monitor the condition of chronically ill patients. AI has also been used to monitor and analyse large datasets on infections and vaccination. Analytical tools used data from mobile apps to track contacts (contact tracing), helping to isolate infected people more quickly, and analysis of social media data allowed the detection of new outbreaks of infection and the study of public sentiment during a pandemic. AI has contributed to the development of precision medicine by analysing individual patient characteristics. AI models supported doctors in making therapeutic decisions, taking into account a patient's age, gender, medical history or laboratory results. BD analytics, on the other hand, allowed risk groups to be identified and medical interventions to be tailored to the population. The pandemic increased the need for psychological support, which resulted in the use of AI in mental health support applications. The tools developed offered online cognitive-behavioural therapies, analysis of the user's emotions based on their responses and tone of voice, and advice on coping with stress and social isolation. In summary, the digital transformation of the health sector using AI was a response to the unprecedented challenges caused by the pandemic. These solutions have not only helped to reduce the impact of the crisis but have also pointed the way for further developments in healthcare technology. However, the future of these developments requires further investment in technology infrastructure, the education of healthcare professionals and the provision of an appropriate legal and ethical framework.

The COVID-19 pandemic forced companies to adapt quickly to changing economic conditions, which accelerated the deployment of AI in business process automation (Żyliński et al. 2024). During the pandemic, the workload on customer service departments increased dramatically, especially in industries such as e-commerce, banking and healthcare services. Customer service automation had to be implemented. AI helped to meet this challenge through chatbots and virtual assistants (NLP-based tools were developed that automatically answered customer questions with quick and precise answers, significantly easing the burden on staff), and AI analysed customer feedback (analysed data from reviews, surveys or social media, helping companies to understand customer needs and tailor the services offered to meet those needs). The disruption to global supply chains caused by the pandemic required AI solutions to minimise waste and increase efficiency. The result is demand prediction (ML algorithms analysed sales data, forecasting product demand in real time), inventory management (AI supported the automation of warehouse processes, such as optimal product placement or inventory control) and route planning (AI systems allowed the most efficient routes for transport to be determined, taking into account changing constraints such as lockdowns or closed borders). Increasing the efficiency of remote working: The forced shift to remote working accelerated the use of AI in human resources management and work organisation. This has resulted in productivity monitoring (AI-based tools analysed employee activity, helping managers assess the effectiveness of remote working), automation of recruitment processes (AI analysed candidates' CVs, conducted initial interviews and helped match the candidate profile to job requirements) and personalisation of employee support (AI offered personalised training and learning materials, supporting the development of competencies in new working environments). The pandemic forced a rapid transition of many companies to digital channels, and AI played a key role in making e-commerce more effective. Effect: Product recommendations (AI systems analysed user preferences, providing personalised product suggestions to increase sales conversions), dynamic pricing (AI algorithms optimised prices in real time, taking into account demand, availability and competitor activity) and fraud detection (AI monitored transactions in real time, identifying suspicious activity and protecting companies from financial loss). Automated reporting and data analysis: Companies struggled to make decisions in an environment of dynamic change, which required rapid access to precise information. The result was real-time data analysis (AI integrated data from a variety of sources, providing managers with comprehensive reports and forecasts in real time), data visualisation (AI tools enabled the creation of interactive dashboards, facilitating the understanding of complex information and decision-making) and reporting automation (AI systems generated cyclical financial, operational or sales reports, saving time and minimising the mistakes that could be made by humans operating under time pressure). Automation using AI helped companies reduce operating costs by replacing routine tasks (AI took over repetitive tasks such as invoice processing, records management or accounting), minimising waste (AI identified areas where the company was losing resources, such as through overproduction or suboptimal operational processes) and energy savings (AI managed energy consumption in office buildings or warehouses, reducing operating costs). In summary, the COVID-19 pandemic was a turning point in business process automation. The rapid deployment of AI not only helped companies to survive difficult times but also enabled them to grow and become more competitive. Continued success in this area will depend on the ability of organisations to integrate new technologies, train employees and invest in innovation.

The COVID-19 pandemic radically changed the approach to education, forcing educational institutions around the world to accelerate the adaptation of AI in remote learning. AI has become a key tool to continue the educational process in new and challenging environments. Personalisation of learning: AI has made it possible to adapt educational content to the individual needs of students. Adaptive learning systems emerged (learning platforms (Dutta et al. 2024) using AI, such as Smart Sparrow or Carnegie Learning, which adapted the difficulty and pace of materials to the student's level of knowledge and learning style), performed progress analysis (AI monitored students' progress, identifying areas for improvement and suggesting appropriate learning materials) and offered personalised support (thanks to AI algorithms, students received suggestions for topics to be repeated or additional exercises). Virtual teachers and assistants: AI has played an important role in replacing some of the functions of teachers in remote environments. Educational chatbots have emerged (tools such as Duolingo Bot and Squirrel AI offered students problem-solving support and answered questions in real time) and automated paper checking (AI systems supported teachers in assessing written work and homework assignments, allowing feedback to be provided more quickly) and simulations and virtual labs (AI enabled interactive online experiments, which was particularly useful in science and engineering). AI has accelerated the creation and distribution of teaching materials. Content generators (AI algorithms were used to automatically create textbooks, quizzes, assignments and presentations), content translation (AI, such as Google Translate or DeepL, enabled the translation of materials into different languages, facilitating learning in international learning environments) and transcription and subtitling (AI platforms automatically generated subtitles for video lessons, supporting students with different needs, such as those with hearing impairments) emerged. AI has significantly increased the efficiency and accessibility of remote education through optimised scheduling (AI algorithms helped to plan lessons, taking into account time differences and student and teacher workloads), interactive learning platforms (AI systems enhanced the learning experience by introducing gamification and interactive quizzes that motivated students to be active) and emotion and engagement recognition (AI analysed students' facial expressions and tone of voice during online lessons, enabling teachers to adapt their approach to lessons). Support for students with special educational needs: AI opened up new possibilities in the education of students with special needs through the development of assistive technologies (AI tools such as speech recognition and text-to-speech conversion systems supported students with literacy difficulties) and the development of personalised learning plans (AI helped to create personalised curricula for students with various disabilities). The pandemic forced students, teachers and parents to quickly master new technological tools, which accelerated the development of digital competences through training in educational tools (AI supported teachers in learning how to use e-learning platforms and other remote learning tools) and learning by doing (students using AI learnt the basics of data analysis, programming and logical thinking, which increased their digital competences). Educational data analysis: AI enabled educational institutions to effectively manage data and make evidence-based decisions by analysing learning outcomes (AI identified trends in educational outcomes, allowing schools and colleges to better plan teaching strategies) and monitoring attendance and engagement (algorithms tracked students' attendance and activity in online classes, helping teachers respond to declines in engagement). In summary, the COVID-19 pandemic accelerated the adoption of AI in education, changing traditional approaches to teaching and opening up new opportunities for both students and teachers. However, the rapid adoption of technology has also revealed challenges, such as the need to ensure access to technology infrastructure, protect personal data and address educational inequalities.

The COVID-19 pandemic has had a huge impact on accelerating the adoption of AI in security and data analytics. The challenges of managing the resulting crisis, protecting data and ensuring security in both remote and cloud-based environments have forced organisations to intensify the deployment of advanced AI solutions. Increased demand for CS: The COVID-19 pandemic has contributed to a surge in cyber threats by increasing the number of attacks. The increase in remote working and migration to the cloud has created new attack surfaces, and cybercriminals have used the pandemic to launch phishing attacks, ransomware and other forms of cyber threats. This has prompted the need to accelerate the deployment of AI in the area of cyber protection through real-time threat detection. AI, including ML-based algorithms, has been used to monitor networks and detect unusual patterns of behaviour that may indicate an attack. These systems learn on the fly and can provide rapid responses to threats. Automatic incident response is another important element. AI-based systems have enabled automatic responses to attacks, such as blocking suspicious IP addresses or isolating infected devices, minimising losses and response times. Privacy and data protection: The increased amount of data collected due to remote working, contact tracking applications and the use of health monitoring tools has led to the need to use advanced AI technologies to manage data. Systems emerged for data pattern recognition

(AI was used to analyse huge datasets to detect data breaches, unauthorised access or information leaks), personal data anomalies (AI systems identified suspicious behaviour in interactions with personal data, helping to identify potential privacy risks) and regulatory compliance management (AI was used to monitor compliance with regulations such as RODO (GDPR), automating the processes involved in analysing, storing and sharing personal data). The pandemic has led to an increased demand for real-time data management, both in the public health context and in the operational context of organisations. Systems (discussed earlier) analysing epidemiological data and asset monitoring systems have emerged. The widespread use of AI to analyse large datasets has led to a better understanding of the impact of the pandemic on societies, economies and different industries. AI algorithms analysed data from multiple sources, such as social media, web searches and mobility data, to predict future changes in consumer behaviour, economics and public health to identify trends. AI enabled the segregation and categorisation of large datasets, facilitating their subsequent use in reports and analysis, and helped make decisions based on real-time data analysis, such as production optimisation, marketing strategy changes or cost reduction decisions. In response to the pandemic crisis, AI supported organisations in automating many business processes related to data management and security. It automatically monitored risk. AI systems analysed security risks in organisations, identifying security vulnerabilities, potential threats from the network or unforeseen security policy incidents, and helped companies automatically monitor and document data security regulatory compliance processes, which became crucial during the pandemic when many companies moved to remote operations. In summary, the COVID-19 pandemic accelerated the adoption of AI in security and data analytics, enabling organisations to identify threats faster, respond to crises and manage data more effectively in real time. These technologies have not only helped in the fight against pandemics but have also pointed the way for the future in the area of data security management and protection against cyber threats. The future of AI in this area will be based on the further development of ML algorithms, integration with IoT systems and ensuring full compliance with data protection and privacy standards.

The transformations that have taken place in logistics and delivery in the wake of the COVID-19 pandemic have been driven by both increased demand for delivery services and the need to optimise processes in the face of pandemic-related disruption. Border closures, transport restrictions and changes in consumer behaviour that necessitated the rapid delivery of goods posed challenges for the logistics sector. In response to these changes, AI has played a key role in route optimisation and fleet management. Algorithms optimised routes in real time (AI, using ML and BDA algorithms, was used to plan the most efficient delivery routes, taking into account changing conditions such as traffic jams, changes in pandemic restrictions or changes in demand for specific products). In addition, they optimised real-time monitoring of transport fleets (thanks to AI, logistics companies were able to monitor their vehicles and check their location, fuel levels, condition and other parameters, allowing them to optimise efficiency and reduce transport costs) and demand forecasting (AI helped predict demand for different products in different locations, allowing the number of vehicles and stock in warehouses to be adjusted). With the increasing number of online orders, especially during pandemic periods, warehouse management has become crucial. AI has helped to automate warehouse processes and increase efficiency. Automated warehouse systems based on AI integrated with robotics in a broad sense allowed automatic sorting, storage and picking of orders in warehouses. AI-assisted robots were able to move goods autonomously, significantly increasing the speed of order fulfilment. In addition, AI predicted the amount of warehouse stock needed, taking into account changing consumer preferences, peak shopping periods (e.g. Black Friday and Christmas) and changing market conditions related to pandemics. Ultimately, AI performed the optimisation of the warehouse space. As a result, companies were able to make better use of warehouse space, increasing storage capacity without having to invest in additional space. Logistics companies began to experiment with delivery robots, drones and autonomous vehicles that were able to deliver parcels to customers without the need for physical interaction with employees. Thanks to AI, logistics companies were able to offer more advanced tracking systems that informed customers of the location of parcels at each stage of transport. These systems used data from GPS, IoT sensors and data analytics to provide accurate information. In summary, the COVID-19 pandemic accelerated the adaptation of AI in logistics and delivery, and changing market conditions and increased e-commerce demands forced companies to implement new technologies. With AI, logistics organisations have been able to optimise their processes, improve operational efficiency and respond faster to changing conditions. In the future, these technologies will become even more advanced, enabling the automation of further areas of logistics, such as returns management or real-time dynamic changes to delivery routes.

The COVID-19 pandemic has had a significant impact on accelerating AI adoption in the labour market (Klonowska et al. 2023). The health crisis, the associated changes in the economy and the needs of the workforce, and the rapid transformation of many industries have forced companies to look for new technological solutions to support their operations, remote working and changing market needs. In this context, AI has played a key role in many aspects of the labour market, both in terms of employment and in terms of the transformation of the way we work. Automation and changes in the nature of work: The introduction of automation of routine tasks – companies that may have previously relied on traditional operational processes have begun to implement AI to automate daily administrative tasks such as data processing, invoicing, customer service (chatbots) and other repetitive tasks. This has allowed companies to save time, reduce operational costs and focus on more valuable tasks that require creativity and analysis. Robotic process automation (Costa et al. 2022) (RPA) is a technology that has grown in importance during the pandemic. With RPA, many companies have been able to automate processes related to data management, customer service, quality control and other tasks, reducing the need for human intervention in day-to-day operations. Increased automation has affected the labour market, changing the requirements for competencies. In many industries, the demand for positions that relied on performing simple, repetitive tasks has decreased, while the need for specialists in new technologies, data management, AI and analytics has increased. AI technologies have supported remote collaboration through platforms that enable automated meeting scheduling, real-time analysis of meeting content (e.g. transcriptions and translations) and organising schedules and tasks. AI improved work organisation, allowing teams to better manage time and tasks, even though team members worked in different locations. Companies began to use AI to monitor the effectiveness of remote working. AI-based tools made it possible to track working time, online activity and task progress. This helped to ensure that employees were appropriately engaged while maintaining the flexibility of remote working. AI also helped to monitor employee well-being. AI-based tools analysed data related to stress levels, fatigue and other aspects of mental health, enabling organisations to offer more personalised interventions to improve employee well-being. Remote learning and skills development have become essential, and AI has played a role in personalising learning pathways. Learning platforms have used AI to tailor materials to individual learners' needs, for example, by analysing learner progress and suggesting appropriate educational content. AI has also become a key tool in automating the creation of training programmes, analysing the skills needed in the labour market and adapting training content to current industry requirements. With the growing demand for AI, cloud computing and data analytics professionals, many companies have invested in courses and curricula that support the development of technical skills. In recruitment processes, AI has made it possible to automate the preselection of candidates, using algorithms to analyse CVs, cover letters and interview data. Pattern recognition technologies enabled recruiters to quickly identify the best candidates for a position. The pandemic accelerated the deployment of AI tools for virtual interviews. Algorithms used facial recognition, body language and voice analysis to evaluate candidates, helping to automatically assess emotional reactions and interpersonal competencies. AI was able to analyse candidates' skills and match them to the required competencies in job advertisements, offering precise recommendations to recruiters. With the growing role of technology, the need for specialists in AI, BDA, CS and data management has increased. Companies have begun to invest in sourcing and developing new talent in these areas. Increased adoption of remote working and migration of processes to the cloud have allowed global marketplace companies to attract talent from all corners of the world. AI has enabled better collaboration and management of global teams. In summary, the COVID-19 pandemic accelerated the introduction of AI into the labour market, changing the way people work, recruit, train and manage. AI has enabled the automation of many processes, increased the efficiency of remote working and aided training and skills development. However, the acceleration of AI adoption in the labour market also raises challenges related to the need to adapt workers' skills to new technologies and the need for an ethical framework to govern the implementation of AI in the employment context.

The COVID-19 pandemic has had a significant impact on accelerating AI adaptation and development in the public sector. Faced with a global health crisis, government administrations around the world were forced to rapidly deploy innovative technological solutions to manage the crisis, ensure continuity of public services and communicate effectively with citizens.

AI has become a key tool in responding to these challenges, supporting both the fight against pandemics and the digital transformation of the public sector. Governments and health organisations around the world have used AI to analyse epidemiological data in real time. AI algorithms helped to model and predict the spread of COVID-19, allowing for better planning of medical resources, testing, hospitalisation and treatment. AI has been used to analyse test results, medical images and patient data, which has contributed to faster diagnosis, especially in the context of uploading PCR test results and analysing lung X-ray scans in real time. Many governments and public organisations have started to use AI systems to monitor the health of citizens. AI-based mobile apps have helped to track symptoms, analyse body temperature and conduct possible medical consultations remotely. AI has been used to automate administrative processes in government agencies. AI algorithms helped with workflows, applications, data analysis and streamlining citizen services, reducing the workload of administrative staff and improving the speed of case processing. AI has been used to forecast demand for public resources such as vaccines, personal protective equipment and hospital beds. Through data analysis, AI was able to predict changes in demand and support effective logistical planning. Governments began using AI-based chatbots and virtual assistants to provide citizens with answers to questions related to COVID-19, quarantine procedures and access to testing or vaccinations. AI also supported access to information about changing legislation and helpful resources, helping to relieve the burden on phone lines and public administration. AI was used to efficiently collect, process and analyse data collected from citizens in the context of a pandemic. AI helped analyse medical, social, economic and health data, enabling accurate predictions and faster administrative decision-making. AI was used to create predictive models to assess the impact of government policies on society, the economy and the health sector. With AI, analysts were able to predict the impact of policies more quickly and effectively and assess the effectiveness of implemented solutions. AI has supported governments in making decisions on the allocation of public funds, especially in the context of the fight against pandemics. It has helped to analyse which areas require immediate support (e.g. healthcare, business support and social assistance) and optimise processes for distributing funds. The public sector has begun to use AI to monitor and detect cyber threats, including attacks on government systems, hospitals or educational institutions. AI has helped to detect anomalies in information systems and respond to security incidents more quickly. Because of the increase in the processing of citizens' health data, AI has been used to protect personal data and ensure compliance with privacy regulations such as RODO. In summary, the COVID-19 pandemic accelerated the adaptation of AI in the public sector, forcing government administrations to rapidly digitise and implement innovative solutions in many areas such as public health, education, crisis management and CS (Klonowska 2023). AI has helped manage crises, supported more efficient delivery of public services and enabled better data-driven decision-making. The application of AI in the public sector has not only improved the quality and speed of response to a health crisis but has also contributed to greater efficiency in public administration.

The COVID-19 pandemic has had a tremendous impact on accelerating the adoption of AI across a number of sectors, including health, education, business and the public sector. In the face of the health crisis, governments and public organisations have begun to make extensive use of AI to monitor the spread of the virus, model predictions of future pandemic development and analyse large medical datasets. AI algorithms helped to diagnose COVID-19 cases faster, as well as to allocate medical resources, such as hospital beds and personal protective equipment, based on predicted needs. In addition, AI has supported processes for tracking contacts of infected individuals and monitoring the health status of citizens, enabling more effective management of quarantines and lockdowns. At the same time, in the public sector, the pandemic forced an accelerated digitalisation of administrative processes. Many public institutions have started to use AI technologies to automate citizen services, including managing applications, processing data and providing information on the pandemic situation. Chatbots and virtual assistants have become popular tools for answering citizens' questions, relieving phone lines and minimising physical contact. AI has also helped to analyse social and economic data, which has supported governments in making decisions on austerity, support for businesses or distribution of funds. In the education sector, AI has become a key tool in organising remote learning. AI-based technologies enabled the personalisation of the educational process, the creation of interactive learning tools and the automation of assessment. With AI, teachers and students were able to use customised learning materials that responded to individual students' needs, improving the quality of distance learning. Remote learning became more accessible, and AI also supported virtual classrooms and activities, providing greater interactivity and student engagement. In the business world, the pandemic has forced an acceleration of digitalisation and automation of processes. AI has played a key role in automating routine tasks, allowing companies to reduce the need for physical contact and convert work to a remote mode. At the same time, in response to changing economic conditions, companies began to use AI to analyse the market, forecast trends and optimise supply chains, allowing them to maintain business continuity in times of uncertainty. Thanks to AI, companies were able to better adapt their strategies to dynamically changing market conditions. Ultimately, the COVID-19 pandemic contributed to the accelerated development and adaptation of AI on various fronts, with its use becoming essential in managing crises, communicating with citizens, organising remote working and transforming traditional processes into digital ones. These transformations have also had long-term implications for the public sector, which has begun to see the benefits of integrating AI into the day-to-day running of government. AI has become a key tool in creating more flexible, automated and resilient public systems that can better respond to future crises and challenges.

2.4 SURVEYS AND RESEARCH: PUBLIC AWARENESS OF AI

Public awareness of AI is becoming a key issue in an era of digital transformation, where this technology is playing an increasingly important role in everyday life. AI is used in many industries, such as health, transport, education, industry and finance, discussed in the previous chapters, making its impact on economies and societies enormous. However, as the technology becomes more complex, there is also a growing need to understand its mechanisms and potential benefits and risks. The aim of the research on public awareness of AI is to explore citizens' knowledge of the technology, their concerns about its introduction and the degree of trust in AI in different areas of life. In particular, it is important to see whether citizens are aware of both the positive aspects of AI, such as increased efficiency in various industries, and the risks associated with its misuse, such as invasion of privacy or the creation of new forms of social inequality. Surveys and research in this area allow for a thorough analysis of societal attitudes, including fears of humans being replaced by machines, fear of losing their jobs or doubts about the ethical issues related to the autonomy of AI systems. Through such research, it is also possible to identify barriers to AI knowledge, which provides a basis for the creation of educational programmes and public policies that promote the development of digital competence in society. Collecting data on the level of public awareness of AI can help develop strategies to manage the development of this technology. For example the results of such surveys can indicate where more education on the benefits of AI is needed, as well as where measures should be taken to mitigate concerns about its negative effects. In addition, surveys can reveal citizens' preferences regarding the legal and ethical regulations that should accompany the introduction of AI into various areas of life. Findings from such surveys can be a valuable source of information for politicians, industry leaders and educational organisations to effectively shape public policies, invest in appropriate educational programmes and introduce regulations that ensure the safe and equitable development of AI. In this way, it is possible not only to minimise public concerns but also to optimise the potential of AI in a way that benefits society as a whole.

The questionnaires are presented below along with the responses. The survey had 516 Polish-speaking respondents and 147 English-speaking respondents.

The questionnaires are presented in Table 2.1. The survey had 516 Polish-speaking respondents marked below PL and 147 English-speaking respondents marked below EN.

The analysis of the results of the survey is on the impact of AI on national security.

The results of the survey indicate a high public awareness of the opportunities and risks of AI. Respondents agree on the need for legal and international regulation, countering disinformation and cyberattacks, educating the public about AI and fostering international cooperation. In both language groups (PL and EN), a consistency of responses and convergence of assessments of key threats and needs is evident.

The full survey is available at the book's web page: <URL TK; Vendor please query PE and AE for URL>.

TABLE 2.1 Survey results

Part I: Analysis of questions 1–13

Question 1. Concept of artificial intelligence (AI)

Polish (PL): AI perceived as an IT tool (64%), technology of the future (51%) and the ability of machines to perform tasks requiring intelligence (47%).

English (EN): Similar answers – IT tool (60%), technology of the future (48%) and machine capabilities (45%).

Conclusion: AI is seen as a practical tool for digital transformation.

Question 2. AI and the development of science and education

PL: 77% positive.

EN: 78% positive.

Conclusion: Consensus on the role of AI in education and science.

Question 3. AI and scientific creativity

PL: 80% supportive.

EN: 81% supportive.

Conclusion: AI supports creativity, not replaces it.

Question 4. AI as a competition to scientific thinking

PL: 58% see AI as competition.

EN: 60% similarly.

Conclusion: Concern about the impact of AI on science.

Question 5. Critical threats to internal security

PL: Disinformation (63%) and cyberattacks (28%).

EN: Disinformation (60%) and cyberattacks (29%).

Conclusion: The biggest threat – manipulation of information.

Question 6. Serious internal threats

PL: New forms of crime (40%) and administration (27%).

EN: New forms of crime (39%) and administration (23%).

Conclusion: Deepfake and manipulation as major threats.

Question 7. Low-level threats

PL: labour market (38%) and AI bugs (28%).

EN: labour market (38%) and AI bugs (31%).

Conclusion: The effects of automation are a real threat.

Question 8. Cyberattacks on the state

PL: 83% recognise the threat.

EN: 86% likewise.

Conclusion: AI as an offensive tool.

Question 9. Disinformation and manipulation

PL and EN: 98% recognise the threat.

(*Continued*)

TABLE 2.1 (Continued)

Conclusion: General agreement.
Question 10. Monitoring and surveillance
PL: 66% positive.
EN: 63% positive.
Conclusion: AI allowed with good regulation.
Question 11. AI and unemployment
PL and EN: 75% expect a problem.
Conclusion: Possible social tensions.
Question 12. Knowledge of regulation
PL: 71% know.
EN: 72% know.
Conclusion: General knowledge and lack of detail.
Question 13. Evaluation of regulation
PL: 60% – insufficient.
EN: 58% – similar.
Conclusion: Need for new solutions.
Part II: Analysis of questions 14–25
Question 14. Critical external threats: Disinformation (PL: 53%; EN: 51%) and autonomous systems (PL: 24%; EN: 30%).
Question 15. Most serious external threats: Terrorism and crime (PL: 41%; EN: 36%) and dependence on foreign AI (PL: 32%; EN: 34%).
Question 16. Low-level threats: Lack of international regulation and destabilisation of the economy.
Question 17. Risk of international conflicts: 77% in both groups say AI increases them.
Question 18. AI cyberattacks: 79% in both groups indicate high risk.
Question 19. AI and global rivalry: The majority consider AI to be a key or important factor.
Question 20. Areas of international rivalry: Cybersecurity, economy and propaganda.
Question 21. Can AI cause international conflicts? Yes/mostly yes: 84% in both groups.
Question 22. International cooperation: EN – 84% in favour; PL – 66% in favour.
Question 23. International organisations: 87% in both groups want them to be more involved.
Question 24. AI training: Social impact, privacy, security and everyday applications.
Question 25. State priorities: Education, infrastructure protection, regulation, monitoring and reduction of technological dependence.

Practical applications of AI in management and education 3

AI is finding increasing applications in management and education, including in areas related to homeland security and sustainability. In the context of governance, AI can significantly support hazard monitoring and prediction by analysing historical accident and disaster data. Systems based on ML algorithms can predict potential risks in mining, public transport or urban infrastructure protection. This enables the relevant services to take preventive action, minimising the impact of emergencies. AI can also support emergency management by analysing weather, geographic and economic data to provide quick recommendations for responding to hazards such as floods or landslides.

In terms of education, AI can support training processes, for example, in health and safety courses for miners and other professional groups. By analysing the progress of learners, AI systems can personalise educational content and adapt the level of difficulty to the individual needs of participants. Virtual hazard simulations allow for realistic replication of emergency situations, which significantly increases the effectiveness of training for emergency services and people working in high-risk environments. In addition, AI can be used to automatically analyse the results of exams and tests, allowing students' knowledge to be assessed more quickly and accurately and teaching methods to be adapted to their needs.

In the area of sustainable mobility, AI supports the analysis and optimisation of public transport, predicting traffic volumes and adjusting timetables to increase the efficiency of public transport. The activities undertaken in the GZM show that the implementation of modern technologies such as AI is key to ensuring safety and sustainability in both governance and education.

DOI: 10.1201/9781003644194-4

3.1 AI AND THOUGHT PROCESSES AND EDUCATION

When thinking about the opportunities and threats presented by AI, attention must be paid to the thinking processes. In the literature, one can find content on the impact of AI on the aforementioned thinking processes. In Sebastian Górski's article "Artificial intelligence is fooling us? Over-reliance on AI interferes with the development of critical thinking?" (Górski 2025), the author puts forward the thesis, which is supported by available research, that the emergence of generative AI may affect the development of an extremely important skill such as critical thinking. This situation is influenced by a kind of uncritical acceptance of information provided by AI.

In the article cited by the author titled "The Impact of Generative AI on Critical Thinking: Self-Reported Reductions in Cognitive Effort and Confidence Effects From a Survey of Knowledge Workers" by Hao-Ping (Hank) Lee, Ian Drosos, Advait Sarkar, Sean Rintel, Nicholas Wilson, Lev Tankelevitch and Richard Banks, describes research on users' perceptions of the impact of generative AI on their own thinking. Areas assessed included precision, clarity, accuracy, breadth, depth, relevance and the meaning or logic of arguments.

The study found that greater trust in AI is simultaneously associated with a decrease in a person's effort in cognitive areas (in terms of knowledge, understanding, analysis, synthesis and evaluation). Although the author of the article himself accuses much of the aforementioned research of being based on Bloom's outdated theory of taxonomy from 1956, the thesis itself is undoubtedly worthy of attention as a potential area to be looked at when considering the possible threats posed by AI.

Equally important are Prof. Aleksandra Przegalińska's theses (Przegalińska et al. 2022) on the existing relationship between the increasing belief in AI's infallibility and the decreasing frequency of checking the news that AI gives us. This is combined with an over-reliance on AI, which can lead to a weakening of analytical skills.

So, can we say that AI weakens critical thinking? If we believe it uncritically, then probably yes, which is rather typical of young AI users. Experienced and mature users are aware of AI's fallibility and do not uncritically believe its data, which they check.

One should not, however, give in to negative thinking about AI, as it is extremely useful in generating content or directing people to the specific knowledge they are looking for. Nowadays, it is not surprising that specialists, scientists and representatives of various professions, preparing specific studies or texts, rely on AI-generated content, which they then verify and correct according to the needs of a given study. The effectiveness of such an action depends on the precision of the questions AI asks. It could be said that, instead of personally collecting materials for a study on a topic, AI is used to find them. Is this a good thing? To some extent, yes, but such "collaboration with AI" raises questions about the topic, or does it lead to a loss of independent thinking, critical thinking and creativity on the part of the creator and the learner?

If the AI user is aware of and co-creates the content with AI that he or she wants to obtain by asking targeted questions, then the generated content is also the result of his or her critical thinking, analysis of the acquired content or the aforementioned creativity.

Reflecting on the thinking processes inherent in the learning process, one must conclude that the peculiar automation of tasks occurring with AI undoubtedly not only speeds up work time but also shifts responsibility for the results obtained to the users of these technologies.

Professor Aleksandra Przegalińska's research is confirmed by the results of other studies available in the literature.

These processes are inextricably linked to education, its effectiveness and the consequences of using AI. Today, we already realise that reality will not be spared the interference of AI in every sphere of it, so it is all the more necessary to be aware of and impart knowledge in this regard, especially to young users.

Lack of critical thinking, problem-solving skills or the ability to select the information we receive means that we are at risk of accepting erroneous content and forming our opinions on it.

AI has irrevocably changed the field of teaching, knowledge transfer and knowledge acquisition. The ease of generating content on an interesting topic without studying it in depth results in intellectual laziness and taking for granted the content received. We can speak here of a kind of "tunnel transmission of information" – narrowly focused content on a specific topic. In the past, when looking for information on a topic, the researcher or student encountered a range of other side information, enriching his or her resources. Being aware of these risks, it is important to take a conscious approach to the use of AI in the educational process.

3.2 AI IN EDUCATION: OPPORTUNITIES AND CHALLENGES

AI in education is opening up new possibilities for education while posing numerous challenges. The use of AI can significantly improve the quality of learning by personalising educational content and adapting it to the individual needs of students. Intelligent learning systems analyse students' progress, identify their strengths and weaknesses and then recommend personalised learning materials. This makes the learning process more effective and tailored to each student's pace and learning style, but over-reliance on AI can lead to a weakening of independence, critical thinking and creativity, which is a major challenge for modern education. Therefore, it becomes crucial to foster in students the ability to use AI tools consciously, critically and responsibly as a support, not as a substitute, for the thought process.

AI also supports the automation of administrative processes in education. It can be used to grade written work and tests and analyse learning outcomes. Automated grading systems allow answers to be checked quickly and objectively, relieving teachers' workload and allowing them to focus on more creative aspects of teaching. In addition, AI can support the management of educational institutions by optimising class schedules, monitoring student attendance and supporting communication among teachers, students and parents.

One of the biggest opportunities related to AI in education is the development of intelligent teaching assistants that can answer students' questions, explain difficult topics and support the learning process in real time. AI can also be used to create virtual learning environments, enabling simulations and interactive learning experiences. Examples include virtual laboratories that allow students to test different scenarios and experiments without the need for physical resources. Contemporary research also points to the potential of AI in police education and professional training, where AI-based simulations can support crisis analysis and real-time decision-making.

Despite the many benefits, implementing AI in education also comes with challenges. One key concern is the need to protect students' personal data and ensure the security of educational systems. AI algorithms process huge amounts of information, so it is important that they are properly secured and not used unethically. Another challenge is to ensure equal access to modern technology so that students from disadvantaged backgrounds can also benefit from AI. There is also a risk of becoming overly dependent on technology and limiting the role of the teacher, which can negatively affect the development of critical thinking skills and human interaction. It is also worth noting the need to adequately prepare teaching staff to work with modern AI tools, which requires additional training and resources.

Education and security (Yu et al. 2023) are closely linked – proper education and awareness-raising of the public contribute to improving security in various dimensions: Digital, social, public and professional. In the context of modern technology and AI, education plays a key role in ensuring the safe functioning of individuals and entire systems. It is the foundation of security. The key roles of security education are to prevent threats (through education on CS, societal risks or responsible use of technology), to learn how to respond to threats (implementation of training in emergency response, risk management and threat analysis) and to raise public awareness (building societal resilience through civic, digital and technical education). The increasing digitisation of education, including the implementation of e-learning, introduces new security challenges. These challenges include an increase in threats such as phishing, ransomware attacks, disinformation or theft of personal data. It is also the safe use of AI in education (AI systems can support education but require appropriate oversight and ethical use) and threat monitoring and analysis (AI tools can detect threats, such as dangerous online content, aggression in schools or plagiarism). AI can support education and security in many ways. The primary ones are personalisation of learning (AI adapts materials to individual students' needs, making education more effective), automatic threat detection (analysing students' behaviour for worrying signals, cyber-bullying and dangerous behaviour), early warning systems (AI can analyse threat data and predict possible incidents in schools or public institutions) and VR/AR simulation and training (using AI in crisis simulations, such as evacuations, cyberattacks or life-threatening situations). Despite the numerous benefits, implementing AI in education carries some risks. We need to focus on privacy and data protection (the collection and processing of student data need to be strictly protected), the ethical use of AI (avoiding biased algorithms and excessive surveillance of students) and limiting reliance on technology (education should not rely solely on AI but support the development of critical thinking and analytical skills). Education is a key component of security, and AI can significantly support this process through personalised learning, threat analysis and early warning systems. However, its implementation requires appropriate regulation and safeguards to ensure data protection and ethical use of the technology.

E-learning platforms (Gligorea et al. 2023) represent a huge opportunity and challenge. The development of e-learning platforms has accelerated in recent years, especially with the COVID-19 pandemic and the global shift to distance learning. Digital education has become standard in many institutions, and its effectiveness depends on modern tools such as AI, data analytics and interactive learning environments. E-learning platforms are learning management systems (LMS) that enable the organisation, delivery and monitoring of the online educational process. They use a variety of technologies. Content management systems (CMS) allow courses to be created and organised. Interactive learning modules quizzes, simulations, video lessons and learning analytics, that is the monitoring of student progress. Integrated communicators allow interaction between teachers and students. The advantages of e-learning platforms are accessibility and flexibility of learning (learning from anywhere and at any time, the ability to adapt the pace of learning to the individual needs of the student and greater accessibility for people with disabilities or limited access to education), personalisation of learning thanks to AI (analysis of the student's progress and adaptation of the content to their level, recommendation systems suggest additional learning materials and automatic generation of tests and individual learning paths) automation and time saving (automatic grading of tests and homework, intelligent chatbots answering students' questions and the ability to analyse students' behaviour and adapt teaching methods) and integration with modern technologies (VR and AR – realistic simulations and interactive online labs, gamification or gamification elements increase student engagement, and BD and analytics to assess teaching effectiveness and predict outcomes). However, these also present challenges and risks. Sensitive student data can be the target of hacking attacks; there is a risk of personal data leakage and monitoring of user activity and the need for strong encryption and authorisation mechanisms. It is also a high dependence on technology. There are problems with technical infrastructure (not every student has access to high-speed Internet and appropriate equipment), possible problems with student concentration and motivation, and the need for teacher training in the use of platforms. Lack of social interaction is also becoming a big problem (online learning can limit the development of social skills, reduce students' engagement in discussions and teamwork and cause challenges in building teacher–student relationships). The future of e-learning platforms is hybrid education (a combination of face-to-face and online learning), the use of advanced AI technologies (increasing the possibility to personalise learning), the development of VR and AR (creating interactive labs, simulations and hands-on online training) and blockchain in education (El Koshiry et al. 2023) (e.g. securing certificates and diplomas from forgery). E-learning platforms are transforming learning by offering accessibility, flexibility and personalisation of education. The use of AI can make learning more effective, but it also brings challenges related to CS, data privacy and reduced social interaction. Finding a balance between technology and traditional teaching methods is key.

3.3 EXAMPLES OF CRISIS MANAGEMENT USING TECHNOLOGY

Modern emergency management (Mount 2023) is increasingly relying on modern technologies to quickly analyse threats, co-ordinate rescue efforts and minimise the impact of disasters. The use of AI, monitoring systems, IoT and e-learning platforms significantly increases the effectiveness of prevention and response activities. Examples of effective emergency management can be found both in urban areas, where intelligent transportation systems support evacuation and traffic management, and in industry, where advanced sensors monitor working conditions, minimising the risk of accidents. Analysing specific cases, such as mining disaster management or natural disaster response, one can see how technology is becoming a key tool in protecting lives and property.

Emergency management in the GZM using technology is monitoring systems and urban mobility management. Intelligent transportation systems are being implemented in the Metropolis to help in emergency situations, such as floods and other natural hazards. They use traffic and public transportation monitoring systems (launched at the Metropolitan Transportation Authority – ZTM) and sustainable urban mobility planning, which takes into account crisis management in emergency situations. Also important is the Metropolitan Development Strategy; the document includes activities related to climate change adaptation, resilience to threats and emergency response plans. The strategy outlines the directions for the GZM and its member municipalities for the coming years for their residents with a view to safety (individual and population), building the resilience of cities/metropolises in various dimensions (natural, infrastructural, economic and social). The factors determining the attractiveness of the municipality/metropolis are important, as well as the functionality of the municipality/metropolis space, determined by accessibility for different groups of residents (Strategia 2023).

Crisis management in the Jastrzębie coal company (JSW) with the use of technology is used in work safety and monitoring of hazards in mines. JSW implements modern technologies to prevent mining accidents using natural hazard monitoring systems by continuously monitoring working conditions and detecting methane and rockburst hazards. It also uses an e-learning training platform for health and safety training for miners. The company has also implemented and launched an online system for safety and crisis management education. Hazard identification systems, occupational risk analysis and emergency response strategies (e.g., methane explosions and mine roadway collapses) have been implemented for industrial disasters.

Examples of historical emergencies in the GZM region: Over the past 30 years, a number of crisis events have occurred in the area that is now the GZM Area. In August 1992, in the area of Kuźnia Raciborska, a fire spread over 9,000 ha of forest, destroyed stands of over 1,160,000 m^3 of timber, scorched the humus layer of the soil and completely destroyed biological life. In 1997, Racibórz was severely affected as part of the so-called flood of the millennium. In 2010, flooding affected many parts of Upper Silesia. Many towns and cities in Cieszyn, Pszczyna, Racibórz and Lubliniec and the western parts of Upper Silesia were flooded. The biggest building disaster in the voivodeship was the collapse of the trade fair hall of the Katowice International Fair. The disaster occurred on 27 January 2006 at around 5.15 pm during a pigeon exhibition in Chorzów. As a result, 65 people died, and more than 170 were injured. On 20–22 July 2007, tornadoes occurred in the vicinity of Częstochowa (Huby, Skrzydlów and Adamów), causing considerable damage. On 16 August 2008, in the districts of Lubliniec and Częstochowa and part of the district of Gliwice, the wind blew the roofs off more than a hundred houses and seriously damaged the existing infrastructure (Walancik 2015). In January 2010, the formation of rime deposited on power cables caused a very large blackout in the area of the Krakow-Czestochowa Jurassic Highlands (in the Zawiercie and Częstochowa districts). Thousands of residents were deprived of energy for several weeks. This was the largest "blackout" phenomenon in Europe. On 3 March 2012, in the village of Chałupki near Szczekociny on railway line No. 64 (Koniecpol-Kozłów), there was a head-on collision between two fast trains. Sixteen people died in the accident. Disasters and damage related to coal mining are characteristic of Upper Silesia.

Today, the GZM region is not just about mines and steel works, but in the past, both the mining and the steel works sectors were the main part of its character. The threat of mining disasters was and is present almost every day in mining work in the Metropolitan region. The long-term consequences of coal mining are, for example, subsidence (e.g. in the Bytom area up to 25 metres), accompanied by cracks in buildings and often collapses. On 10 January 1990, a methane explosion occurred at the Halemba coal mine in Ruda Śląska. Nineteen miners were killed, and 20 were injured (Katastrofa 1990). On 21 November 2006, a methane explosion occurred at the Halemba coal mine in Ruda Śląska. The methane explosion initiated a coal dust explosion. The mining disaster resulted in the deaths of 23 miners (eight employees of the mine and 15 employees of a company cooperating with the mine). It was one of the most tragic mining disasters in Poland (Katastrofa 2006). On 23 April 2202, at the "Zofiówka" mine in Jastrzębie-Zdrój belonging to the "Borynia-Zofiówka" joint-venture mine JSW, a mining disaster occurred as a result of a high-energy shock combined with a methane explosion (Katastrofa 2022). The disaster resulted in the deaths of ten miners.

According to the report, published by the Higher Mining Authority, there was a 0.3% increase in total mining accidents in 2022 compared to 2021, that is, from 2,078 to 2,085 accidents. This was influenced by a 2.6% increase in the number of accidents in coal mining, from 1,773 accidents occurring in 2021 to 1,819 accidents occurring in 2022 (Wypadki 2022). In hard coal mining, the number of fatal accidents increased from nine accidents occurring in 2021 to 22 accidents occurring in 2022. There was also an increase in the number of severe accidents from three accidents in 2021 to 12 accidents in 2022. Impact on fatal and severe accidents in coal mining in 2022 (WypadkiWUG 2022): The fatal and severe accident rate in this sector was significantly affected by the disasters that occurred in 2021 in the mines of JSW.

Recently, large holes and fissures of varying depths, for example 10 m, resulting from ground collapse, have become a hazard in many localities in the region (Jaworzno, Olkusz, Ruda Śląska and Świętochłowice). Large holes and fissures (Szczeliny 2022) are formed in areas where coal mines operated and mining took place. Arguably, the dynamic process of closing mines during the transformation period took place with disregard for the rules of decommissioning and safeguarding. The selected examples of crisis situations presented affect the sense of security of the region's inhabitants. Below, on the basis of a case study, the solutions proposed by the entities of the GZM (JSW and the GZM itself) to increase safety are presented.

3.4 CASE STUDY: GZM

The analysis presented here uses the case study method (case study and case analysis). A case study is a research method that includes a broad description of a certain social phenomenon (Ragin & Becker 1992). The aim of this method is the exploration, in-depth analysis, evaluation and description (Babbie 2001) of selected cases, allowing conclusions to be drawn about the causes and results of its course and cultural and social (Pietrzak & Baran 2007). It is a qualitative study that can span multiple disciplines. Through the use of multiple techniques of data collection and analysis, it allows solving scientific and practical problems (Grzegorczyk 2022). The main research problem of the studied social action took the form of the question: How is sustainable development implemented in the area of social security in JSW and in sustainable urban mobility in the Metropolis?

The geographic–historical–social location of the GZM: In the context of the subject of exploration, it is worthwhile to refer to and indicate the location and conditions of the Metropolis in the broader geographical, historical and social context, which is the region of the Silesian Voivodeship known as Upper Silesia and the Dąbrowa Basin.

It is from the area of the Silesian Voivodeship that the GZM was created. The Silesian Voivodeship – with an area of 12,333.09 km^2 – stretches across the Silesian Lowlands, the Silesian-Cracow Uplands, the Oświęcim Basin and the West Beskid Mountains. It covers the eastern part of Upper Silesia and the western part of western Lesser Poland, including the Zagłębie Dąbrowskie, the western Zagłębie Krakowskie, the Żywiec region and Częstochowa. It is inhabited by some 4,375,947 people. The Silesian Voivodeship is the unit with the highest degree of urbanisation and population density in Poland. The voivodeship was first established in the Second Republic. Historically, it comprises the lands of Upper Silesia, part of Lesser Poland and Greater Poland.

It was in the Upper Silesian conurbation area that the GZM was established on 1 July 2017 on the basis of a decree of the Council of Ministers, pursuant to the Act of 9 March 2017 (Decree of the Council of Ministers of 26 June 2017, Journal of Laws 2022, item 1709). The GZM has a territorial and an institutional dimension. The territory is the area of 41 member municipalities, covering about 50% of the population of the Silesian Voivodeship and about 20% of its area. The institution is positioned between the local and regional levels. The organisational structure of the GZM is:

- GZM Assembly: The decision-making and controlling body (one delegate from each member municipality);
- GZM Management Board: The executive body (five members, including the chairman; one representative from each subregion);
- Metropolitan Office: Performing the tasks commissioned by the GZM Management Board (Development Strategy of the GZM for 2022–2027 with an Outlook to 2035, 2023, pp. 9–10). It is the only legally established metropolitan association in Poland. The Metropolis lies on the route of major national and international routes, both by road and by rail. The Katowice-Pyrzowice international airport operates in the north of the Metropolis. The Metropolis is an economic centre. It is a commercial and service centre with a significant share of manufacturing activities. It is also a centre of concentration of specialised medical services and academic, cultural, religious and sports functions. The association started its activities at the beginning of 2018. It receives funds for its activities from the state budget – a 5% share of PIT from persons living in the area of the association, as well as contributions from the budgets of the municipalities that form it.

The Silesian Voivodeship borders two countries (the Slovak Republic and the Czech Republic) and four voivodeships – the Łódzkie, Małopolskie, Opolskie and Świętokrzyskie voivodeships. It was created from the former Bielsko-Biala, Częstochowa and Katowice voivodeships as part of the country's administrative reform. The voivodeship covers an area of 12,333.09 km and is home to 4.62 million people or 12.1% of the country's population. The population density is 377.4 per km^2, making it the highest in Poland. The area ranks 14th out of 16 voivodeships, while in terms of population, it is the second most populous voivodeship after the Masovian Voivodeship (Walancik 2007).

It has 71 cities, including 19 cities with powiat status. It is characterised by a significant share of national minorities (German, Czech and Moravian). In the central part of the voivodeship is the Upper Silesian Industrial District (GOP), which is the most heavily industrialised area in Poland, and smaller industrial districts such as the Częstochowa Industrial District.

The key plants include industrial coal mines (currently 20), steel works and power plants (currently 22). The voivodeship has a very well-developed air transport infrastructure with the Katowice-Pyrzowice international airport, rail transport with a modern railway station in Katowice, through which EuroCity and InterCity trains pass, and road infrastructure with the A1 and A4 motorways. The A4 and A1 motorways, which intersect here, connect the west with the east and the north with the south of our continent. In addition, there are expressways in the region: S 1, S 69, S 86 and numerous national roads, provincial roads and cross-city roads (DTŚ). Public transport was solved by the Communal Transport Union of the Upper Silesian Industrial Region (KZK GOP) and the Municipal Transport Enterprises (Municipal Transport Company). Currently, public transport is organised on the territory of the cities belonging to the metropolitan association and the neighbouring municipalities (a total of 56 cities and municipalities) by the Metropolitan Transport Authority, ZTM – the organisational unit of the GZM.

The year 1989 and subsequent years were a special period for Europe and Poland in terms of the political, social and economic transformation of the Upper Silesian and Zagłębie Dąbrowskie regions. After that year, the most radical changes took place in the fields of politics, economics and social life. On 1 January 1990, a package of laws regulating the new rules for all economic entities came into force. This date can be taken as the beginning aimed at the reconstruction of the economy and ownership relations. The transformation of the system extended to groups of employees who had enjoyed special protection under the previous system. Among the first to experience the changes were employees of the State Agricultural Farms (PGR), definitely to a lesser extent in the Upper Silesia region than in Pomerania. Subsequently, miners, the social group most characteristic of the region, felt the acute changes. The restructuring of individual industries came down to the closure of plants or a drastic reduction in employment among production workers. From June 2002 to March 2004, the privatisation process of Polskie Huty Stali SA (Polish Steelworks) was completed. In February 2005, Mittal Steel Poland SA was registered (Meszyński & Walancik 2013). Subsequently, the existing plants were modernised, new investment works were started and the production specification was changed. During this period, the situation of steel-workers stabilised to a certain extent. It appears that the many years' process of restructuring the coal industry, taking into account optimisation of the level and structure of output, undertakings to increase productivity and concentration of production, improvement of sales efficiency, rationalisation of investment policy, employment, finance and organisation, stabilised the situation in the sector in the final years of the last decade of the twentieth century. As part of the restructuring, JSW was established on 1 April 1993, as a company wholly owned by the State Treasury, and on 29 June 1993, the Katowice Coal Holding Joint Stock Company (KHW S.A.) was established in Katowice. On 1 February 2003, "Coal Company Joint Stock Company" in Katowice was established on the basis of five coal companies. On 16 January 2015, it was established (under the name of Polska Grupa Górnicza sp. z o.o.) to take over the assets and liabilities of the bankrupt coal company.

Arrangements of the developed Development Strategy for the Upper Silesian-Zagłębów Metropolis for 2022–2027 with an outlook to 2035 are in line with contemporary trends and needs, constituting priorities such as adaptation to climate change and resilience, activities according to the principles of sustainable development, mobility and accessibility, space and social cohesion metropolitanship and innovation. The GZM Development Strategy sets out the directions for the GZM and its member municipalities for the coming years, for their inhabitants, bearing in mind safety (individual and population) and building the resilience of the cities/metropolises in various dimensions (natural, infrastructural, economic and social). The factors determining the attractiveness of a municipality/metropolis are important, as well as the functionality of the municipality/metropolis space determined by accessibility for various groups of inhabitants (Development Strategy of the GZM 2022–2027 with an Outlook to 2035, 2023).

Ensuring state security is a complex process dependent on many external and internal factors. Maintaining the state's security at an appropriate level necessitates interdepartmental cooperation involving government administration, local government administration, entrepreneurs and state institutions. Such cooperation has a special dimension in the territory of a territorial self-government unit such as a voivodeship, especially a metropolis. Entities implementing tasks in the area of national security in the voivodeship are located on several levels of management. These activities are carried out at the municipal (city), district, voivodeship and departmental level, as well as at the metropolitan level.

A classic example of sustainability and safety measures in the mining sector is the action taken by JSW, the largest entity in the region and in the country in terms of coal mining and employment. According to research and analysis, the sector has recently recorded the highest fatal and severe accident rates (Wypadki 2022).

Sustainability at JSW in the area of safety concerns safety and health protection within the JSW group: Safety measures are treated on a par with production or economic performance. In the case of occupational health and safety (OHS) management, the objective is to reduce the number of incidents which endanger life and health.

The group's strategy sets, among other things, the following tasks in the area of health and safety:

- continuous monitoring and prevention of natural hazards and working conditions,
- ensuring the high technical level of the plants,
- maintaining a certified OHS management system for mining, processing and sale of coal,
- maintaining a high quality of OHS training, with particular emphasis on the topicality and practicality of the issues discussed,
- raising awareness of OHS (web-based training and information platform "The Foreman's Zone and beyond"),
- taking action to prevent accidents, occupational illnesses and near misses and
- taking measures to limit the spread of the SARS-CoV-2 virus (Raport 2021).

As part of the "Integrated Management System Policy", the management of JSW undertakes to ensure that the necessary measures and resources are in place to create safe attitudes among employees and to monitor risks and limit their impact on the work environment. An important activity is the systematic improvement of employees' qualifications. Key procedures related to OHS include the following:

- hazard identification and occupational risk assessment (PZB-7.01),
- accidents at work, occupational diseases and near misses (PZB-7.02),
- monitoring of OHS (PZB-8.01) and
- actions at JSW S.A. during a mass accident or industrial disaster (PZB-8.02).

Other procedures defining the principles of operational management important for employee issues are as follows:

- human resources management (PSZ-6.01),
- internal and external communication (PSZ-5.02) and
- dealing with emergencies, for example epidemic, biological or chemical threats (PSB-8.03).

With a view to improving working conditions and protecting the health of employees, it is important to identify hazards and assess occupational risks carried out directly at JSW's plants. Occupational risk assessment for individual job groups is carried out by a team of employees with the necessary knowledge of:

- assessing the occupational risks,
- identifying hazards at the workstations being assessed,
- assessing the harmful consequences of the hazards present and
- identifying and selecting preventive measures.

The risk assessment process is carried out in accordance with the procedure "Identification and assessment of occupational risk" as part of the integrated management system. Sustainable development in JSW in the area of safety concerning safety and health protection in the JSW Group due to working conditions in JSW's mines included an extended scope of preventive medical examinations in the field of occupational medicine. In order to reduce the exposure of JSW's mine workers to factors causing occupational diseases (pneumoconiosis, hearing damage, chronic musculoskeletal diseases and vibration syndrome), mine-based preventive programmes for occupational hearing damage and pneumoconiosis are in operation with the participation of the Institute of Occupational Medicine and Environmental Health in Sosnowiec, as well as mine-based OHS services and doctors providing occupational medicine care. In 2021, in connection with the COVID-19 pandemic, OHS activities and initiatives were also aimed at preventing the spread of the SARS coronavirus – CoV 2.

In order to ensure a high level of health and safety knowledge and appropriate professional qualifications for employees, a plan for health and safety training and upskilling courses is being implemented at all JSW plants. In view of the pandemic situation, a JSW e-learning platform was established in 2021.

The JSW e-learning platform created to conduct periodic health and safety training for established groups of JSW and JSW SIG employees in the form of self-directed learning using electronic communication means and the Internet is working and functioning very well.

Classic examples of sustainable safety activities are sustainable mobility in the Metropolis. The problem of mobility in the Metropolis from a safety point of view is crucial. The territory of the cities belonging to the metropolitan association and the neighbouring municipalities (a total of 56 cities and municipalities) is the largest area for a public transport organiser in Poland. Today, mobility issues in the region are managed by the Metropolitan Transport Authority, ZTM – an organisational unit of the GZM.

The process of developing the new sustainable urban mobility plan (SUMP) is based on dialogue with citizens and those responsible for mobility in the municipalities. In order to increase the transparency of the process, as well as the possibility of verifying the actions taken, a Modern Mobility Council was established in the Metropolis, consisting of representatives of municipalities, scientists, service providers and representatives of non-governmental organisations (Mobilność 2019).

Properly organised public transport is not only a common ticket for trains, buses and trams, comfortable public transport, allowing you to get to work, school, shopping or the cinema efficiently, but it is also the development of cycling infrastructure and modern railways.

Thus, the key to sustainable mobility in the Metropolis is rail transport. In the future, it is to be the backbone of the entire public transport system in the Metropolis. For this to happen, the Metropolitan Railway needs to be built. The first stage in the construction of the railway was a concept, which was developed between 2018 and 2019. It contained four options for the development of the railway – from the basic to the most extensive.

After its preparation, the document was consulted with the Marshal of the Silesian Voivodeship, the Silesian Voivode, PKP PLK S.A. and representatives of the cities and municipalities of the GZM, as well as entities related to the railway market. Postulates and suggestions made by stakeholders as part of the consultations carried out were analysed by experts from the Silesian University of Technology, and a supplement to the Metropolitan Railway Concept was created, in which modified railway development options were developed.

The second stage involved the preparation of a document titled "Preliminary Feasibility Study of the Metropolitan Railway in the GZM" (Kolej 2019).

The document contained detailed data on the costs of investment for individual options. A detailed description of the course of the individual routes and the location of the new railway stops was presented, which is crucial from the point of view of public safety.

To sum up, today's world and region are full of actors participating in the implementation of security policy. Thus, security research from a multifaceted and interdisciplinary perspective seems to be a natural activity.

In the institutions of the modern state, holistic and interdisciplinary research relating to the solution of security problems and, in particular, actions for its sustainable development is the main driving force for the development of theory in the social sciences, including security research.

The cases selected and presented on the basis of a case study in the Upper Silesian-Gazovian Metropolis are part of sustainable development measures. They are in line with the directions of the GMC, bearing in mind the safety (individual and population) of its residents, the attractiveness of the Metropolis and the functionality of the metropolitan space, which is characterised by its accessibility for various groups of residents.

The concept of sustainable development, and in particular that encompassing activities in the area of safety, is gaining more and more supporters. It is being implemented in many countries/regions. The basis of the concept of sustainability is people as agents of the environment in which they live, which is the micro subject of our planet as an area of human influence. In this concept, the method of action is partnership. This is because it allows for integrated action and, consequently, the solution of the problems of the inhabitants to achieve the objective of the concept, namely, secure development and world peace. After all, as H. Komiyama and K. Takeuchi write, it is in the concept of sustainable development that a strong emphasis is placed not only on the elimination of barriers to growth, poverty, the implementation of innovative solutions and the growth of intangible assets but also on the protection of the environment and the possibility of renewing resources, which is particularly important in the new global conditions (Komiyama & Takeuchi 2006).

3.5 OPPORTUNITIES AND LIMITATIONS OF TECHNOLOGY IN SECURITY MANAGEMENT

AI is changing the way organisations are managed (Kłoczko 2024), automating processes, analysing data and supporting decision-making. Today's businesses and public institutions are increasingly using AI to optimise operations, increase efficiency and improve service delivery. With the ability to process massive amounts of data, AI enables better strategy planning and more accurate business decisions. The opportunities, potential benefits and possibilities of using AI in management include improved efficiency, time savings, better decision-making and innovative approaches to organisational management. By using AI, companies can react faster to market changes, optimise processes and increase their competitiveness.

AI reduces costs and eliminates routine tasks, for example, in records management or customer service. Automated systems can respond to customer queries, manage databases or even generate reports, significantly easing the burden on employees. Analysing large datasets makes it possible to anticipate market changes and make better decisions. AI can analyse customer behaviour patterns and, based on this, suggest directions for the company, which helps to adapt strategies to changing market conditions. It can also customise products, services and management strategies. In e-commerce, AI systems analyse users' preferences and recommend products to them, leading to increased sales and customer satisfaction. It optimises logistical, manufacturing and operational processes, reducing errors and minimising task times. In manufacturing, for example, AI can monitor the condition of machines and predict the need for maintenance, preventing breakdowns and reducing downtime. AI algorithms analyse available data and provide managers with comprehensive reports to help make strategic decisions. AI can identify the most effective solutions based on the analysis of thousands of possible scenarios.

However, management is not only about opportunities but also about limitations. Sophisticated AI systems require significant investment, both for implementation and for subsequent maintenance and updating of the algorithms. AI management requires skilled professionals who can design, implement and supervise AI-based systems. Automated decision-making can lead to problems with process transparency and a lack of control over algorithms. There is a risk that AI systems will act unpredictably or may lead to unintended consequences, such as discrimination in recruitment processes or credit assessment. AI is based on the data that are fed into it, so incorrect, incomplete or biased data can lead to incorrect decisions.

AI in education (Zalewska-Bochenko 2024) opens up new possibilities for both students and teachers. The introduction of AI into the educational system allows the learning process to be tailored to individual students' needs, improves assessment and supports the development of competencies in a more effective and interactive way. The potential facilities and opportunities that AI offers to teachers and students include better organisation of the learning process, individualisation of the approach to the student and increased efficiency of knowledge acquisition.

AI makes it possible to adapt the pace and difficulty level of material to the individual needs of the student. By analysing progress, AI can suggest additional learning materials or adjust the learning path according to performance. It can administer tests, check written work and provide real-time feedback. Automating assessment allows teachers to focus on more advanced aspects of teaching, rather than spending time routinely checking tests. Intelligent chatbots and AI assistants can act as tutors, answering students' questions, explaining more difficult topics or conducting interactive lessons. AI can analyse student performance and identify those with learning difficulties. Systems can suggest to teachers which students require additional support and which strategies might be most effective for them. With AI, it is possible to create educational content tailored to people with disabilities, such as speech recognition systems for the visually impaired or automatic translations for students learning in another language. But, of course, there are not only advantages but also limitations. Over-reliance on AI in education can lead to a reduction in the teacher–student relationship, which is crucial for social development. AI analyses huge amounts of data about students, which raises the risk of invasion of privacy and unauthorised use of information. It can also generate erroneous or unverified information, which can lead to misinformation and teaching errors. Over-reliance on AI in education can lead to problems when systems fail or technology is unavailable.

The opportunity to use technology in security management is seen in the ability to analyse huge datasets, identifying patterns and predicting potential threats, enabling faster and more effective preventative action, supporting the analysis of camera footage, identifying suspicious behaviour, enabling rapid response to threats and supporting crisis management by analysing the situation in real time and suggesting the best operational actions, as well as helping to profile perpetrators or analyse links between criminal incidents. In contrast, we see the limitations of new technologies in security management in the use of monitoring, which can lead to surveillance and violations of civil rights. AI can make mistakes in identifying people or situations, which can lead to wrongful accusations, while advanced AI-based security systems require significant financial investment.

AI has great potential in governance, education and security, but it requires appropriate regulation, standards and investment in CS. The implementation of the technology should take ethical considerations into account and ensure control of the algorithms to minimise the risk of misuse.

4 Summary and conclusions

AI is becoming the foundation of modern digital transformation in almost all sectors of social and economic life. Its potential in terms of processing huge amounts of data, automating decision-making processes and learning from patterns means that AI not only accelerates digital transformation but also makes it more effective and adapted to dynamically changing conditions. Key areas where AI can play a strategic role include education, management and public safety. In the education sector, AI enables the personalisation of the teaching process by adapting teaching materials to the level and needs of a specific pupil or student. AI also supports teachers by automating test grading, analysing the effectiveness of teaching methods and proposing solutions to improve the quality of education. In higher and specialist education (e.g. police training), AI can also be used to simulate crisis situations, conduct training in VR or analyse operational data for teaching purposes. In management, both in the public and private sectors, AI serves as a tool supporting decision-making processes. It enables the forecasting of trends (e.g. migration, economic and demographic), the optimisation of resource allocation (e.g. human, financial and material) and the automation of administrative and reporting processes. Thanks to the use of AI in management systems, it is possible to create so-called smart institutions, flexible organisations that respond quickly to changes, are resilient to crises and are better prepared for future challenges. In the area of public safety, AI has enormous potential in monitoring public spaces (e.g. facial recognition and real-time threat identification), analysing intelligence and operational data (e.g. to detect criminal networks and analyse crime patterns), predicting threats and supporting decision-making in crisis situations. AI can also support preventive measures, for example by analysing online behaviour (hate speech, radicalisation), and improve the management of emergency situations (e.g. natural disasters and cyberattacks). AI is not only the technology of the future, but it is also a real tool supporting social development, improving the quality of education, management efficiency and public safety. Its integration with digital processes is becoming an indispensable element of modern development strategies for both public and private institutions. The key challenges in this context are the ethical and secure implementation of

DOI: 10.1201/9781003644194-5

AI, building digital competencies and ensuring transparency and public trust in intelligent systems.

Despite its enormous potential, the development of AI also carries serious risks that could negatively impact public safety, social stability and citizens' trust in institutions. One of the most significant challenges is the phenomenon of disinformation, which is taking on new, more advanced forms, thanks to the capabilities of generative AI. The creation of realistic but completely false content, such as deepfakes, fabricated videos or manipulated images, can be used to spread panic, destabilise public opinion, interfere in electoral processes or deliberately destroy the reputation of public figures. In a geopolitical context, this technology is becoming a tool of information warfare. The second serious threat is cyberattacks, which are becoming more effective thanks to the support of AI systems. AI enables cybercriminals to create malware in an automated manner, carry out advanced phishing campaigns tailored to specific victims and bypass security measures in real time. With their ability to analyse large datasets, algorithms can also identify the weakest points in organisational structures and security systems, making attacks more precise and difficult to detect. It is also worth noting the risk of job losses as a result of advancing automation. Many sectors of the economy, especially administration, manufacturing, transport and trade, may be dominated in the coming years by AI-based solutions that will perform tasks faster, cheaper and without error. If appropriate retraining and social support programmes are not implemented, this could lead to an increase in unemployment, the professional marginalisation of people with low digital skills and a deepening of socio-economic inequalities. One of the most controversial aspects of AI development is the risk of its misuse. AI-based systems can operate in a non-transparent manner, and their algorithms, if not properly supervised, can reproduce or even reinforce biases and stereotypes present in the input data. In the hands of irresponsible actors, AI can be used for mass surveillance of citizens, for example, through facial recognition systems installed in public spaces without public consent or for automated decision-making in justice, recruitment or social welfare systems. Particularly worrying are scenarios involving the use of AI in autonomous weapons systems, where the decision to use lethal force could be left to a machine. In summary, the development of AI must be balanced by a responsible regulatory approach, the development of ethical standards for the design of AI systems, public education and the provision of effective oversight mechanisms. Only in this way will it be possible to minimise the risks and threats while maximising the benefits of this groundbreaking technology.

The results of the survey clearly indicate growing public awareness of AI, both in terms of its enormous potential and the real risks it poses. More and more citizens recognise that AI can significantly improve everyday life – from medicine and education to transport and security – but at the same time, there is an understanding of the risks associated with misinformation, job losses, privacy violations and unethical use of data. Respondents point out that the dynamic development of AI cannot take place in a regulatory vacuum. It is necessary to create clear, precise and internationally consistent regulations that will ensure the transparency of AI systems, the protection of human rights and the possibility of holding entities that abuse this technology accountable. Public institutions and the private sector are also expected to act responsibly, taking into account not only profit but also the social and ethical consequences of implementing algorithms. The research also reveals a strong belief in the need for universal education in AI. Society should be not only a user of new technologies but also a conscious participant in the digital transformation process. Digital education, both at school and in continuing education, should cover not only technical skills but also critical thinking, the ability to recognise information manipulation and an understanding of the basics of how AI systems work. Emphasising the importance of education and regulation is one of the most important conclusions drawn from observing social reactions to the development of AI today. Only an aware and prepared society will be able to not only reap the benefits of AI but also effectively protect itself from its undesirable effects.

In view of the dynamic development of AI-based technologies, the need for consistent, comprehensive legal and ethical regulations is becoming increasingly apparent. The lack of a clear legal framework may lead to the uncontrolled development of AI systems, which has serious social, economic and political consequences. Contemporary states and international organisations face the challenge of creating regulations that, on the one hand, do not stifle innovation and, on the other hand, effectively limit the risk of abuse, discrimination, privacy violations and threats to democracy and public safety. Regulations should include, among other things, transparency of algorithms, the possibility of auditing them and the obligation to inform users that they are dealing with an AI-based system. It is also important that responsibility for decisions made by AI is not blurred but clearly assigned to specific entities, creators, operators or users of a given system. Only in this way will it be possible to maintain public trust in new technologies and protect the fundamental rights of citizens. Equally important are ethical regulations, which should go hand in hand with legal provisions. AI systems must be designed and implemented in a way that takes into account values such as human dignity, equality, justice, privacy and non-discrimination. Mechanisms are needed to prevent algorithmic bias and measures to enable users to appeal against decisions made automatically by AI. Particular caution should be exercised when applying AI in sensitive sectors such as justice, recruitment, healthcare and internal security. Given the global nature of AI technology, regulations cannot be exclusively national. International cooperation is necessary to harmonise standards, exchange good practices and effectively control the cross-border use of AI. Initiatives such as the EU AI Act, the work of the OECD and the actions of the UN show that the international community recognises the importance of the issue, but the world still faces many challenges related to the implementation and enforcement of common rules. In summary, the importance of legal and ethical regulations in the context of AI cannot be overestimated today. Only through a responsible and consistent regulatory approach will it be possible to exploit the full potential of AI while minimising risks and protecting the public interest.

Contemporary education faces the challenge of adapting to the realities of the information society, in which AI plays an increasingly important role. AI can and should support teaching processes by facilitating the personalisation of teaching, the analysis of student progress and the automation of certain administrative tasks. Modern education systems successfully use algorithms to create customised learning paths, interactive materials and intelligent tutors. However, despite all these benefits, it should not be forgotten that the main goal of education is not only to convey information but also to develop critical thinking skills, intellectual independence and civic responsibility. AI should not replace these competencies but support them. Over-reliance on technology can lead to a weakening of the ability to independently analyse, reason and evaluate information – and these are precisely the skills that are crucial in a world overloaded with data and threatened by misinformation. That is why it is so important that education not only uses AI as a tool but also teaches how to use this technology consciously and responsibly. In this context, the development of citizens' digital competences becomes a key element, not only technical skills such as the use of IT tools but also soft skills: Recognising manipulation, assessing the credibility of sources, understanding the basics of how algorithms work and awareness of the risks associated with the processing of personal data. These competences should be developed from the early stages of formal education and continued as part of lifelong learning for adults. Education therefore plays a key role in preparing society for life in a world dominated by algorithms and automation. Only a well-educated, aware and critically thinking society will be able to harness the potential of AI in a responsible manner while avoiding the pitfalls of its ill-considered implementation.

AI is increasingly influencing the shape of modern security systems, both internal and external. It can serve as a powerful tool to strengthen a state's ability to protect its citizens and respond to threats, but at the same time, if misused or falling into the wrong hands, it can contribute to the destabilisation of public order and even weaken state sovereignty. From an internal security perspective, AI is used for advanced analysis of operational and intelligence data, threat forecasting, identification of potential perpetrators of crimes and recognition of crime patterns. AI-based systems can support the activities of services in real time, for example by monitoring public spaces, detecting suspicious behaviour, analysing social media posts or processing emergency calls more quickly. In the context of terrorist threats, organised crime and cybercrime, AI can significantly increase the effectiveness of preventive and operational activities. AI is equally important for external security. This technology is playing an increasingly important role in defence, including through strategic analysis systems, autonomous reconnaissance and combat platforms and cyber defence systems. At the same time, however, AI is also becoming a tool for waging new forms of conflict. Contemporary cyberwars are fought not only in the IT network but also in the information sphere – through automated disinformation, fake news and manipulation of social narratives. AI can be used to massively influence public opinion, undermine trust in state institutions or destabilise the socio-political situation, both nationally and internationally. This dual nature of AI, on the one hand as a tool for increasing control and security and on the other hand as a potential threat, requires special attention from institutions responsible for national security. It is essential not only to implement modern technologies in security and defence structures but also to develop the ability to counter the use of AI by hostile actors, both state and non-state. In summary, AI is today one of the key factors influencing the architecture of national security. Its potential can be used both to protect citizens and as a tool of aggression. That is why it is so important that the development of this technology proceeds in a responsible manner, under the control of democratic institutions and in accordance with international security standards.

Due to the cross-border nature of AI-related challenges, close and consistent international cooperation is essential. AI, like other digital technologies, develops in a global environment – data, algorithms and applications know no national borders, and potential threats such as cyberattacks, disinformation or the unethical use of autonomous systems can have effects that extend beyond the jurisdiction of a single country. Therefore, countries and international organisations must work together to create a coherent legal, ethical and technical framework that will ensure the safe, responsible and fair development of AI. Only through the harmonisation of norms and standards will it be possible to effectively monitor the use of AI in various sectors and prevent abuse. This applies in particular to areas such as privacy, human rights, data security, algorithm transparency and responsibility for decisions made by autonomous systems. International cooperation also includes the exchange of information and good practices among countries, scientific institutions, the private sector and non-governmental organisations. This allows for the building of mutual trust, strengthening the ability to respond to threats and jointly developing technological solutions in line with universal values. Examples of such initiatives include the European Union's actions under the AI Act, the OECD guidelines on responsible AI and the United Nations' efforts to develop global principles for autonomous weapon systems. A common approach is particularly important in the face of the technological race between global powers. Competition for dominance in the field of AI must not lead to the disregard of safety standards and human rights. It is therefore necessary to build an international consensus based on shared values, not solely on geopolitical interests. In summary, international cooperation on regulation, standardisation and information exchange on AI is not a luxury but a necessity. Only joint action by the international community will enable the sustainable development of this groundbreaking technology while maintaining peace, security and the rule of law on a global scale.

The development of AI brings not only enormous potential but also serious challenges in terms of digital security. With the growing scale of data processing and process automation, the attack surface that cybercriminals, hacker groups or hostile state actors can exploit is increasing. Therefore, progress in AI must be closely linked to the parallel development of data protection systems, critical infrastructure and incident response procedures. Investments in CS should include both modern defence technologies and the development of specialist skills. The protection of critical infrastructure, such as energy networks, transport systems, financial institutions, healthcare and public administration, requires the implementation of advanced monitoring systems, early threat detection and automatic attack neutralisation. AI can play the role of both a shield and a sword here, on the one hand increasing the effectiveness of defence systems and on the other hand being a tool in the hands of cybercriminals, which forces a constant increase in the level of security. Data security is also of key importance, as data is the fuel for AI systems. Its unauthorised acquisition or modification can lead to serious consequences, including manipulation of algorithm results or theft of strategic information. Therefore, investments should include, among other things, the development of encryption, access control systems, data anonymisation and mechanisms to ensure the integrity and authenticity of information. Human factors cannot be overlooked either. Even the most advanced security systems will be ineffective if employees are not properly trained in cyber hygiene and incident response. Investments in CS must therefore also include educational programmes, raising awareness of threats and simulation exercises to prepare for potential attacks. In summary, the development of AI and CS are processes that should run in parallel. Only through systematic investment in protective technologies, infrastructure and human skills can the risk of attacks, abuse and destabilisation caused by the illegal or unethical use of AI be minimised.

The development of AI is not only a matter of technological progress but also a profound ethical and social challenge. The widespread implementation of AI can have a significant impact on the structure of society, the labour market and relations between citizens and institutions. Therefore, it is essential that progress in this field is consistent with the principles of sustainable development and serves the common good, rather than solely the interests of a narrow group of economic or political entities. One of the key risks is the marginalisation of certain social groups. Process automation can lead to job losses in sectors particularly susceptible to the replacement of humans by machines, which in turn can exacerbate economic and social inequalities. If the digital transformation is not supported by appropriate education and retraining programmes, many people may find themselves outside the labour market, leading to their exclusion from economic and social life. Another challenge is the risk of algorithmic bias, that is, a situation in which AI systems reproduce or reinforce existing biases present in the data on which they learn. This can result in discrimination based on, among other things, gender, ethnic origin, economic status or place of residence. To counteract this, it is essential to ensure the transparency of algorithms, their regular auditing and the participation of interdisciplinary teams, bringing together specialists in the fields of technology, law, sociology and ethics, in the process of designing and implementing AI systems. From a social perspective, it is also important to ensure that the benefits of AI development are widely distributed and accessible to different social groups, not just the most privileged. AI should support equal opportunities, improve the quality of public services, increase access to education and healthcare, and strengthen social bonds, rather than contributing to their erosion. In summary, the development of AI must be conducted in an ethical, responsible and inclusive manner. This requires not only legal regulations but also conscious social policy-making that will prevent marginalisation and promote solutions based on the principles of justice, equality and solidarity. Only then will AI become a tool for genuinely supporting the common good, rather than a source of new divisions.

In order for AI to develop in a safe, responsible and beneficial way for society, it is necessary to set out clearly defined courses of action covering legal, ethical, educational and technological aspects. The first and key area is legal regulation, which should create a coherent national and international framework ensuring the transparency of AI systems, the protection of citizens' rights and the possibility of holding entities accountable for using the technology in an unlawful or unethical manner. Harmonising regulations and adapting them to the global nature of AI-related challenges will be the foundation for the safe development of this technology.

An equally important direction is the ethics of technology, understood as the creation and implementation of AI systems based on values such as equality, justice, respect for human dignity, transparency and accountability. This requires algorithm audits, eliminating bias in data and involving interdisciplinary teams in the design and implementation of AI-based solutions. The third pillar of action should be public education. The development of citizens' digital competences, critical thinking skills and the ability to use new technologies consciously is essential for AI to become a tool that supports development rather than a source of exclusion. Education should cover all age groups, from primary school pupils to senior citizens, as well as continuing vocational training programmes. Another direction is to support the development of innovation. The state and the private sector should invest in research and development in the field of AI to create modern, competitive and secure solutions. Cooperation among science, business and administration can accelerate the implementation of technologies that are also compliant with legal and ethical standards. The last but equally important area is building the resilience of security systems. AI must be developed in parallel with advanced solutions in the fields of CS, data protection and critical infrastructure security. This includes both investments in protective technologies and training for specialists responsible for responding to incidents and preventing attacks. In summary, the future of AI depends on the parallel development of legal regulations, technology ethics, education, innovation and security. Only an integrated approach covering these areas will allow the full potential of AI to be exploited while minimising risks and protecting the public interest.

Announcement of a series of studies and publications

Two unique books devoted to the key challenges of contemporary training in uniformed services will be published soon.

The first, titled "Research on the level of digital competence of uniformed services officers in Poland", is a comprehensive analysis of the digital skills of officers in the police, border guard, State Protection Service and State Fire Service. The results of the study will show how well-prepared individual groups are to work in the digital age and where new training solutions are needed.

The second – "Study of the level of adaptation of e-learning in police training and its impact on the quality of training" – will show how modern online teaching methods are changing the training of officers. Based on data analysis, surveys and interviews, the publication will indicate how to increase the effectiveness and attractiveness of e-learning in police education.

Both titles combine reliable research with a practical look at the needs of the forces responsible for national security, offering specific conclusions and recommendations for decision-makers, trainers and researchers.

Bibliography

Abawajy, J. (2015). Comprehensive analysis of big data variety landscape. *International Journal of Parallel, Emergent and Distributed Systems*, 30(1), 5–14.

Alaba, F. A. (2024). The evolution of the IoT. In *Internet of Things: A case study in Africa* (pp. 1–18). Cham: Springer Nature Switzerland.

Alaei, M., & Yazdanpanah, F. (2024). A survey on heterogeneous CPU – GPU architectures and simulators. *Concurrency and Computation: Practice and Experience*, e8318.

Ali, M. H., Jaber, M. M., Alfred Daniel, J., Vignesh, C. C., Meenakshisundaram, I., Kumar, B. S., & Punitha, P. (2023). Autonomous vehicles decision-making enhancement using self-determination theory and mixed-precision neural networks. *Multimedia Tools and Applications*, 1–24.

Ali, Z. A., Atia, T. S., Yousuf, A. Y., & Khahdim, A. J. (2024). A comprehensive review of quantum image encryption methods: Design characteristics, cryptographic properties, and AI integration. *Quantum Information Processing*, 23(10), 335.

AllahRakha, N. (2024). UNESCO's AI ethics principles: Challenges and opportunities. *International Journal of Law and Policy*, 2(9), 24–36.

Al-Shareeda, M. A., Saare, M. A., Manickam, S., & Karuppayah, S. (2023). Bluetooth low energy for internet of things: Review, challenges, and open issues. *Indonesian Journal of Electrical Engineering and Computer Science*, 31(2), 1182–1189.

Arena, F., Pau, G., & Severino, A. (2020). An overview on the current status and future perspectives of smart cars. *Infrastructures*, 5(7), 53.

Armstrong, G., Martino, C., Rahman, G., Gonzalez, A., Vázquez-Baeza, Y., Mishne, G., & Knight, R. (2021). Uniform manifold approximation and projection (UMAP) reveals composite patterns and resolves visualization artifacts in microbiome data. *mSystems*, 6(5), 10–1128.

Asadi, M., Jamali, M. A. J., Heidari, A., & Navimipour, N. J. (2024). Botnets unveiled: A comprehensive survey on evolving threats and defense strategies. *Transactions on Emerging Telecommunications Technologies*, 35(11), e5056.

Aslan, Ö., Aktuğ, S. S., Ozkan-Okay, M., Yilmaz, A. A., & Akin, E. (2023). A comprehensive review of cyber security vulnerabilities, threats, attacks, and solutions. *Electronics*, 12(6), 1333.

Astobiza, A. M., Toboso, M., Aparicio, M., & López, D. (2021). AI ethics for sustainable development goals. *IEEE Technology and Society Magazine*, 40(2), 66–71.

Attia, A. A., Liu, J., Ai, W., Demszky, D., & Espy-Wilson, C. (2024, October). Kid-whisper: Towards bridging the performance gap in automatic speech recognition for children vs. adults. In *Proceedings of the AAAI/ACM conference on AI, ethics, and society* (Vol. 7, pp. 74–80).

Atzeni, D., Bacciu, D., Mazzei, D., & Prencipe, G. (2022). A systematic review of Wi-Fi and machine learning integration with topic modeling techniques. *Sensors*, 22(13), 4925.

Babbie, E. (2001). *The practice of social research*, 9th Edition. Belmont, Wadsworth Thomson.

Bajal, E., Katara, V., Bhatia, M., & Hooda, M. (2022). A review of clustering algorithms: Comparison of DBSCAN and K-mean with oversampling and t-SNE. *Recent Patents on Engineering*, 16(2), 17–31.

Balamurali, M. (2023). T-Distributed stochastic neighbor embedding. In *Encyclopedia of mathematical geosciences* (pp. 1527–1535). Cham: Springer International Publishing.

Barman, A., Deb, B., & Chakraborty, S. (2020). A glance at genome editing with CRISPR – Cas9 technology. *Current Genetics*, 66, 447–462.

Batalov, E., Haverstock, P., Anderson, R., Thompson, W., & Wolverton, R. (2024). Ransomware detection via network traffic analysis using isolation forest and LSTM neural networks. *Authorea*. October 18, 2024. DOI: 10.22541/au.172928576.69686584/v1

Beaman, C., Barkworth, A., Akande, T. D., Hakak, S., & Khan, M. K. (2021). Ransomware: Recent advances, analysis, challenges and future research directions. *Computers & Security*, 111, 102490.

Bernstein, D. J., & Lange, T. (2017). Post-quantum cryptography. *Nature*, 549(7671), 188–194.

Bisong, E., & Bisong, E. (2019). Google bigquery. In *Building machine learning and deep learning models on google cloud platform: A comprehensive guide for beginners* (pp. 485–517). Apress.

Blagoveshchenskaya, M. M., Ngongang, R. D., & Blagoveshchenskiy, I. G. (2022). Structure of project xml format. In Информатизация и автоматизация в пищевой промышленности. *Тип: статья в сборнике трудов конференции Язык: английский Год издания. Страницы* (pp. 109–115).

Boorugu, R., & Ramesh, G. (2020, July). A survey on NLP based text summarization for summarizing product reviews. In *2020 Second international conference on inventive research in computing applications (ICIRCA)* (pp. 352–356). IEEE.

Borchers, N., Clark, S., Horstmann, B., Jayasayee, K., Juel, M., & Stevens, P. (2021). Innovative zinc-based batteries. *Journal of Power Sources*, 484, 229309.

Bukowski, M., & Klonowska, I. (2024). Boskie AI. Sztuczna inteligencja i edukacja. Poszukiwanie nowych horyzontów w kontekście edukacyjnym, teologicznym i technologicznym – szanse i zagrożenia. *Kościół i Prawo*, 13, 151–168. https://doi.org/10.18290/kip2024.24.

Buteau, E., & Lee, J. (2021). Hey Alexa, why do we use voice assistants? The driving factors of voice assistant technology use. *Communication Research Reports*, 38(5), 336–345.

Cao, K., Liu, Y., Meng, G., & Sun, Q. (2020). An overview on edge computing research. *IEEE Access*, 8, 85714–85728.

Cao, Y., Li, S., Liu, Y., Yan, Z., Dai, Y., Yu, P. S., & Sun, L. (2023). A comprehensive survey of AI-generated content (AIGC): A history of generative ai from GAN to ChatGPT. *arXiv preprint* arXiv:2303.04226.

Cartwright, O., Dunbar, H., & Radcliffe, T. (2024). Evaluating privacy compliance in commercial large language models-ChatGPT, Claude, and Gemini. In Review. https://doi.org/10.21203/rs.3.rs-4792047/v1.

Chauhan, A. (2019). A review on various aspects of MongoDB databases. *International Journal of Engineering Research & Technology (IJERT)*, 8(05), 90–92.

Chen, R., & Goldberg, J. H. (2020). Actor-critic reinforcement learning in the songbird. *Current Opinion in Neurobiology*, 65, 1–9.

Chen, T., Li, M., Li, Y., Lin, M., Wang, N., Wang, M., . . . Zhang, Z. (2015). Mxnet: A flexible and efficient machine learning library for heterogeneous distributed systems. *arXiv preprint* arXiv:1512.01274.

Cheng, X., Li, Y., Kou, J., Liao, D., Zhang, W., Yin, L., . . . Ma, L. (2022). Novel non-nucleic acid targets detection strategies based on CRISPR/Cas toolboxes: A review. *Biosensors and Bioelectronics*, 215, 114559.

Chiu, T. K. (2023). The impact of Generative AI (GenAI) on practices, policies and research direction in education: A case of ChatGPT and Midjourney. *Interactive Learning Environments*, 1–17.

Chrzanowska, S., & Plewa, P. (2023). Broń biologiczna – czy należy się jej bać? Epidemiologia, metody produkcji i cele ataku. *ELIXIR*, I, 19–32.

Chung, S., Moon, S., Kim, J., Kim, J., Lim, S., & Chi, S. (2023). Comparing natural language processing (NLP) applications in construction and computer science using preferred reporting items for systematic reviews (PRISMA). *Automation in Construction*, 154, 105020.

Ciotti, M., Ciccozzi, M., Terrinoni, A., Jiang, W. C., Wang, C. B., & Bernardini, S. (2020). The COVID-19 pandemic. *Critical Reviews in Clinical Laboratory Sciences*, 57(6), 365–388.

Clifton, J., & Laber, E. (2020). Q-learning: Theory and applications. *Annual Review of Statistics and Its Application*, 7(1), 279–301.

Costa, D. A. D. S., Mamede, H. S., & Silva, M. M. D. (2022). Robotic Process Automation (RPA) adoption: A systematic literature review. *Engineering Management in Production and Services*, 14(2).

Daher, Z., & Hajjdiab, H. (2018). Cloud storage comparative analysis amazon simple storage vs. Microsoft azure blob storage. *International Journal of Machine Learning and Computing*, 8(1), 85–9.

Daley, A. J., Bloch, I., Kokail, C., Flannigan, S., Pearson, N., Troyer, M., & Zoller, P. (2022). Practical quantum advantage in quantum simulation. *Nature*, 607(7920), 667–676.

Danopoulos, D., Kachris, C., & Soudris, D. (2018, May). Acceleration of image classification with Caffe framework using FPGA. In *2018 7th international conference on modern circuits and systems technologies (MOCAST)* (pp. 1–4). IEEE.

Darmawikarta, D. (2007). Dimensional data warehousing with MySQL: A tutorial. *Brainysoftware.com*. https://brainysoftware.com/home

David, A., Islam, S., Tankhilevich, E., & Sternberg, M. J. (2022). The AlphaFold database of protein structures: A biologist's guide. *Journal of Molecular Biology*, 434(2), 167336.

Davidson, G. P., & Ravindran, D. D. (2021). Technical review of Apache Flink for big data. *International Journal of Aquatic Science*, 12(2), 3340–3346.

Davidson, J. (2017). *Apple Homekit: The beginner's guide* (Vol. 1). Van Helostein.

Dehouche, N., & Dehouche, K. (2023). What's in a text-to-image prompt? The potential of stable diffusion in visual arts education. *Heliyon*, 9(6).

Developers, T. (2022). *TensorFlow*. Zenodo.

Dolot, A. (2018). The characteristics of generation Z. *E-mentor*, 74(2), 44–50.

Durner, D., Leis, V., & Neumann, T. (2021, June). JSON tiles: Fast analytics on semi-structured data. In *Proceedings of the 2021 international conference on management of data* (pp. 445–458).

Dutta, S., Ranjan, S., Mishra, S., Sharma, V., Hewage, P., & Iwendi, C. (2024, February). Enhancing educational adaptability: A review and analysis of AI-driven adaptive learning platforms. In *2024 4th international conference on innovative practices in technology and management (ICIPTM)* (pp. 1–5). IEEE.

Eisner, S. P. (2005). Managing generation Y. *SAM Advanced Management Journal*, 70(4).

El Koshiry, A., Eliwa, E., Abd El-Hafeez, T., & Shams, M. Y. (2023). Unlocking the power of blockchain in education: An overview of innovations and outcomes. *Blockchain: Research and Applications*, 4(4), 100165.

Eriksson, J., & Newlove-Eriksson, L. M. (2023). Outsourcing the American space dream: SpaceX and the race to the stars. *Astropolitics*, 21(1), 46–62.

Farahani, B., Firouzi, F., & Chakrabarty, K. (2020). Healthcare IoT. In *Intelligent Internet of Things: From device to fog and cloud* (pp. 515–545). Springer.

Fatollahi Arani, S., & Zeinoddini, M. (2023). Gene editing: Biosecurity challenges and risks. *Journal of Police Medicine*, 12(1), 1–19.

Feng, D. (2019, March). Review of quantum navigation. In *IOP conference series: Earth and environmental science* (Vol. 237, p. 032027). IOP Publishing.

Fitria, T. N. (2023). Augmented reality (AR) and virtual reality (VR) technology in education: Media of teaching and learning: A review. *International Journal of Computer and Information System (IJCIS)*, 4(1), 14–25.

Fradkov, A. L. (2020). Early history of machine learning. *IFAC-PapersOnLine*, 53(2), 1385–1390.

French, R. M. (2000). The Turing Test: The first 50 years. *Trends in Cognitive Sciences*, 4(3), 115–122.

Frenkel, D., & Smit, B. (2023). *Understanding molecular simulation: From algorithms to applications*. Elsevier.

Frøland, H. I., Palm, E., Kralevska, K., & Gligoroski, D. (2023, October). Web3 and blockchain for modernizing the reseller market. In *2023 fifth international conference on blockchain computing and applications (BCCA)* (pp. 215–220). IEEE.

Gai, R., Du, X., Ma, S., Chen, N., & Gao, S. (2021, March). A summary of 5G applications and prospects of 5G in the Internet of Things. In *2021 IEEE 2nd international conference on big data, artificial intelligence and Internet of Things engineering* (ICBAIE) (pp. 858–863). IEEE.

Garvey, S. C. (2021). The "general problem solver" does not exist: Mortimer Taube and the art of AI criticism. *IEEE Annals of the History of Computing*, 43(1), 60–73.

Ghosal, A., Nandy, A., Das, A. K., Goswami, S., & Panday, M. (2020). A short review on different clustering techniques and their applications. *Emerging Technology in Modelling and Graphics: Proceedings of IEM Graph 2018*, 69–83.

Gisin, N., Ribordy, G., Tittel, W., & Zbinden, H. (2002). Quantum cryptography. *Reviews of Modern Physics*, 74(1), 145.

Gligorea, I., Cioca, M., Oancea, R., Gorski, A. T., Gorski, H., & Tudorache, P. (2023). Adaptive learning using artificial intelligence in e-learning: A literature review. *Education Sciences*, 13(12), 1216.

Glöckler, J., Sedlmeir, J., Frank, M., & Fridgen, G. (2024). A systematic review of identity and access management requirements in enterprises and potential contributions of self-sovereign identity. *Business & Information Systems Engineering*, 66(4), 421–440.

Gnad, D., Gotthard, M., Krautter, J., Kritikakou, A., Meyers, V., Rech, P., . . . Traiola, M. (2024, May). Reliability and security of AI hardware. In *2024 IEEE European test symposium (ETS)* (pp. 1–10). IEEE.

Góra, T. (2023). Zarządzanie kryzysowe na szczeblu gminnym – wybrane zagadnienia. *Prawo i Bezpieczeństwo*, (1), 32–37.

Górniak, D., & Kopniak, P. (2017). Porównanie szybkości działania wybranych funkcji skrótu i algorytmów szyfrowania. *Journal of Computer Sciences Institute*, 4.

Grieves, M., & Hua, E. Y. (2024). Defining, exploring, and simulating the Digital Twin metaverses. In *Digital twins, simulation, and the metaverse: Driving efficiency and effectiveness in the physical world through simulation in the virtual worlds* (pp. 1–31). Cham: Springer Nature Switzerland.

Grosse-Oetringhaus, J. F., Quishpe, R., Abramyan, A., Cruceru, R., & Grigoras, C. (2023). *The hyperloop train system (No. ALICE-PUBLIC-2023–005)*. ALICE Collaboration.

Grzegorczyk, W. (2022). Studium przypadku jako metoda badawcza i dydaktyczna w naukach o zarządzaniu. [w:] W. Grzegorczyk (red.), *Wybrane problemy zarządzania i finansów. Studia przypadków*. Łódź: Wydawnictwo Uniwersytetu Łódzkiego.

Gu, S., Yang, L., Du, Y., Chen, G., Walter, F., Wang, J., & Knoll, A. (2022). A review of safe reinforcement learning: Methods, theory and applications. *arXiv preprint* arXiv:2205.10330.

Gupta, M. P. (2018). Google assistant controlled home automation. *International Research Journal of Engineering and Technology*, 5(5).

Haenlein, M., & Kaplan, A. (2019). A brief history of artificial intelligence: On the past, present, and future of artificial intelligence. *California Management Review*, 61(4), 5–14.

Halegoua, G. (2020). *Smart cities*. MIT Press.

Hasan, B. M. S., & Abdulazeez, A. M. (2021). A review of principal component analysis algorithm for dimensionality reduction. *Journal of Soft Computing and Data Mining*, 2(1), 20–30.

Hasan, S. R., Chowdhury, M. Z., Saiam, M., & Jang, Y. M. (2023). Quantum communication systems: Vision, protocols, applications, and challenges. *IEEE Access*, 11, 15855–15877.

Hauben, M. (2007). History of ARPANET. *Site de l'Instituto Superior de Engenharia do Porto*, 17, 1–20.

He, B., Ismail, N., Leng, K. K. K., & Chen, G. (2023). Techno-economic analysis of an HRES with fuel cells, solar panels, and wind turbines using an improved Al-Biruni algorithm. *Heliyon*, 9(12).

Hidary, J. D., & Hidary, J. D. (2021). A brief history of quantum computing. In *Quantum computing: An applied approach* (pp. 15–21). Springer.

Howard, J., & Gugger, S. (2020). Fastai: A layered API for deep learning. *Information*, 11(2), 108.

Hu, J., & Szymczak, S. (2023). A review on longitudinal data analysis with random forest. *Briefings in Bioinformatics*, 24(2), bbad002.

Hughes, M. E., & Angela, M. O. (2004). *The lives and times of the baby boomers*. New York: Russell Sage Foundation.

Hussain, A., Mohamed, A., & Razali, S. (2020, March). A review on cybersecurity: Challenges & emerging threats. In *Proceedings of the 3rd international conference on networking, information systems & security* (pp. 1–7).

Ikotun, A. M., Ezugwu, A. E., Abualigah, L., Abuhaija, B., & Heming, J. (2023). K-means clustering algorithms: A comprehensive review, variants analysis, and advances in the era of big data. *Information Sciences*, 622, 178–210.

Ikromovna, A. Z. (2023). SQL (structured query language) capabilities of the statistical database language. *Multidisciplinary Journal of Science and Technology*, 3(5), 274–280.

Imambi, S., Prakash, K. B., & Kanagachidambaresan, G. R. (2021). PyTorch. In *Programming with TensorFlow: Solution for edge computing applications* (pp. 87–104). Cham: Springer International Publishing.

Jacobsen, J. T. (2021). Cyber offense in NATO: Challenges and opportunities. *International Affairs*, 97(3), 703–720.

Jaeger, T. (2022). *Operating system security*. Springer Nature.

Jain, S. M. (2022). Hugging face. In *Introduction to transformers for NLP: With the hugging face library and models to solve problems* (pp. 51–67). Berkeley, CA: Apress.

Jasudowicz, T. (2001). Klonowanie człowieka – z perspektywy standardów Rady Europy. *Medycyna Wieku Rozwojowego*, 5(1).

Jiang, L., Liu, D. Y., & Yang, B. (2004, August). Smart home research. In *Proceedings of 2004 international conference on machine learning and cybernetics (IEEE Cat. No. 04EX826)* (Vol. 2, pp. 659–663). IEEE.

Jiang, R., Banchs, R. E., & Li, H. (2016, August). Evaluating and combining name entity recognition systems. In *Proceedings of the sixth named entity workshop* (pp. 21–27). Association for Computational Linguistics.

Jiang, W., & Schotten, H. D. (2021, December). The kick-off of 6G research worldwide: An overview. In 2021 *7th international conference on computer and communications (ICCC)* (pp. 2274–2279). IEEE.

Joshi, S. A. (2024). Simplifying infrastructure management with terraform and YAML configuration. Vaasan Ammattikorkeakoulu University of Applied Sciences. Cloud-Based Software Engineering.

Jouppi, N., Kurian, G., Li, S., Ma, P., Nagarajan, R., Nai, L., . . . Patterson, D. A. (2023, June). Tpu v4: An optically reconfigurable supercomputer for machine learning with hardware support for embeddings. In *Proceedings of the 50th annual international symposium on computer architecture* (pp. 1–14). Association for Computing Machinery.

Kalbfleisch, M. L., & Banasiak, M. (2008). ADHD. In J. A. Plucker & C. M. Callahan (Eds.), *Critical issues and practices in gifted education: What the research says* (pp. 15–30). Prufrock Press Inc.

Kamionka, M. (2023). *Rosyjska wojna hybrydowa w mediach społecznościowych na przykładzie*. Wiedza Obronna.

Kelley, P. G., Yang, Y., Heldreth, C., Moessner, C., Sedley, A., Kramm, A., . . . Woodruff, A. (2021, July). Exciting, useful, worrying, futuristic: Public perception of artificial intelligence in 8 countries. In *Proceedings of the 2021 AAAI/ACM conference on AI, ethics, and society* (pp. 627–637). Association for Computing Machinery.

Kellokoski, J., Koskinen, J., & Hämäläinen, T. (2014). Always best connected heterogeneous network concept. *Wireless Personal Communications*, 75, 63–80.

Kepuska, V., & Bohouta, G. (2018, January). Next-generation of virtual personal assistants (Microsoft Cortana, Apple Siri, Amazon Alexa and Google Home). In *2018 IEEE 8th annual computing and communication workshop and conference (CCWC)* (pp. 99–103). IEEE.

Kessler, G. C. (2004, December). An overview of TCP/IP protocols and the internet. *InterNIC Document*, 29, 42.

Khan, W., Kumar, T., Zhang, C., Raj, K., Roy, A. M., & Luo, B. (2023). SQL and NoSQL database software architecture performance analysis and assessments – a systematic literature review. *Big Data and Cognitive Computing*, 7(2), 97.

Kim, S., Jeon, H., Koo, J. M., Oh, D. X., & Park, J. (2024). Practical applications of self-healing polymers beyond mechanical and electrical recovery. *Advanced Science*, 11(16), 2302463.

Kitahara, I., Kogure, K., & Hagita, N. (2004, August). Stealth vision for protecting privacy. In *Proceedings of the 17th international conference on pattern recognition, 2004* (Vol. 4, pp. 404–407). IEEE.

Kleczkowska, A. (2023). Autonomous weapons and the right to self-defence. *Israel Law Review*, 56(1), 24–40.

Klonowska, I. (2023). Wyższa Szkoła Policji w Szczytnie w pandemii COVID-19 – problemy, wyzwania, rozwiązania systemowe. Perspektywa edukacyjna i logistyczna. [w:] I. Klonowska, E. Kuczyńska, & P. Gawroński (red.), *Covid-19 a funkcjonowanie uczelni wyższych i szkół o profilu policyjnym. Dokąd zmierzamy?* (s.15–28). Toruń: wyd. Adam Marszałek.

Klonowska, I., Żyliński, A., Płaczek, A., & Gawroński, P. (red.). (2023). *Nowe zjawiska w dobie pandemii Covid-19. Implikacje społeczne*. Szczytno.

Kłoczko, A. (2024). Wykorzystanie sztucznej inteligencji w zarządzaniu organizacją jako potencjał obniżenia kosztów. *Zeszyty Naukowe Politechniki Częstochowskiej. Zarządzanie*, 1(55), 61–77.

Komiyama, H., & Takeuchi, K., (2006). Sustainability science: Building a new discipline. *Sustainability Science*, (1).

Kramer, O., & Kramer, O. (2016). Scikit-learn. In *Machine learning for evolution strategies* (pp. 45–53). Springer.

Kumar, S. N. (2015). Review on network security and cryptography. *International Transaction of Electrical and Computer Engineers System*, 3(1), 1–11.

Kumari, P., & Jain, A. K. (2023). A comprehensive study of DDoS attacks over IoT network and their countermeasures. *Computers & Security*, 127, 103096.

Kunduru, A. R. (2023). Blockchain technology for ERP systems: A review. *American Journal of Engineering, Mechanics and Architecture*, 1(7), 56–63.

Kupperschmidt, B. R. (1998). Understanding generation X employees. *JONA: The Journal of Nursing Administration*, 28(12), 36–43.

Ladd, T. D., Jelezko, F., Laflamme, R., Nakamura, Y., Monroe, C., & O'Brien, J. L. (2010). Quantum computers. *Nature*, 464(7285), 45–53.

Lakshika, T., & Caldera, A. (2022). Association rules for knowledge discovery from e-news articles: A review of Apriori and FP-growth algorithms. *Advances in Science, Technology and Engineering Systems Journal*, 7(5), 178–192.

Lane, J. E. (2021). *Understanding religion through artificial intelligence: Bonding and belief*. Bloomsbury Publishing.

Li, T., Badre, A., Alambeigi, F., & Tavakoli, M. (2023). Robotic systems and navigation techniques in orthopedics: A historical review. *Applied Sciences*, 13(17), 9768.

Li, Q., Zuo, D., Feng, Y., & Wen, D. (2024). Research on high-performance Fourier transform algorithms based on the NPU. *Applied Sciences*, 14(1), 405.

Li, Y., Hsu, E. B., Pham, N., Davis, X. M., Podgornik, M. N., & Trigoso, S. M. (2022). Developing public health emergency response leaders in incident management: A scoping review of educational interventions. *Disaster Medicine and Public Health Preparedness*, 16(5), 2149–2178.

Lopatovska, I., Rink, K., Knight, I., Raines, K., Cosenza, K., Williams, H., . . . Martinez, A. (2019). Talk to me: Exploring user interactions with the Amazon Alexa. *Journal of Librarianship and Information Science*, 51(4), 984–997.

Lyu, K., & Hao, M. (2021). Definition and history of smart cities: The development of cities and application of artificial intelligence technology in smart cities. In *AI-based services for smart cities and urban infrastructure* (pp. 1–22). IGI Global.

Ma, C., Li, J., Wei, K., Liu, B., Ding, M., Yuan, L., . . . Poor, H. V. (2023). Trusted AI in multiagent systems: An overview of privacy and security for distributed learning. *Proceedings of the IEEE*, 111(9), 1097–1132.

Manaswi, N. K., & Manaswi, N. K. (2018). Understanding and working with Keras. In *Deep learning with applications using Python: Chatbots and face, object, and speech recognition with TensorFlow and Keras* (pp. 31–43). Apress.

Marques-Cruz, M., Dias, D. M., Fonseca, J. A., & Sousa-Pinto, B. (2024). Ten year citation prediction model for systematic reviews using early years citation data. *Scientometrics*, 129(8), 4847–4862.

Martens, J. (2020). New insights and perspectives on the natural gradient method. *Journal of Machine Learning Research*, 21(146), 1–76.

McIntosh, T., Kayes, A. S. M., Chen, Y. P. P., Ng, A., & Watters, P. (2021). Ransomware mitigation in the modern era: A comprehensive review, research challenges, and future directions. *ACM Computing Surveys (CSUR)*, 54(9), 1–36.

Meszyński, K., & Walancik, M. (red.). (2013). *Współdziałanie terenowych organów administracji wojskowej administracji województwa w sytuacjach kryzysowych.* Warszawa: Stowarzyszenie Ruch Wspólnot Obronnych.

Meyer, M. (2020). Biohacking. In *The handbook of peer production* (pp. 211–224). Wiley.

Miao, Q., Zheng, W., Lv, Y., Huang, M., Ding, W., & Wang, F. Y. (2023). DAO to HANOI via DeSci: AI paradigm shifts from AlphaGo to ChatGPT. *IEEE/CAA Journal of Automatica Sinica*, 10(4), 877–897.

Mir, S. H., Ashruf, S., Bhat, Y., & Beigh, N. (2019). Review on smart electric metering system based on GSM/IOT. *Asian Journal of Electrical Sciences*, 8(1), 1–6.

Morandín-Ahuerma, F. (2023). Twenty-three Asilomar principles for artificial intelligence and the future of life. OSFpreprints. https://osf.io/preprints/osf/dgnq8_v1 https://doi.org/10.31219/osf.io/dgnq8 September 12, 2023 Center for Open Science.

Motie, S., & Raahemi, B. (2024). Financial fraud detection using graph neural networks: A systematic review. *Expert Systems with Applications*, 240, 122156.

Mount, J. F. (2023). *California rivers and streams: the conflict between fluvial process and land use*. Univ of California Press.

Mrożek, Ż. (2023). Bioterroryzm jako zagrożenie dla bezpieczeństwa państwa. *Przegląd Geopolityczny*, (45), 150–165.

Murdick, D., Dunham, J., & Melot, J. (2020). *AI definitions affect policymaking*. CSET Issue Brief. Center for Security and Emerging Technology.

Naeem, S., Ali, A., Anam, S., & Ahmed, M. M. (2023). An unsupervised machine learning algorithms: Comprehensive review. *International Journal of Computing and Digital Systems*, 13, 911–921. 10.12785/ijcds/130172.

Naser, S. M. (2021). Cryptography: From the ancient history to now, it's applications and a new complete numerical model. *International Journal of Mathematics and Statistics Studies*, 9(3), 11–30.

Nikitin, P. V., Rao, K. V. S., & Lazar, S. (2007, March). An overview of near field UHF RFID. In *2007 IEEE international conference on RFID* (pp. 167–174). IEEE.

Offert, F. (2023). On the concept of history (in foundation models). In: IMAGE. Zeitschrift für interdisziplinäre Bildwissenschaft. Generative Imagery: Towards a 'New Paradigm' of Machine Learning-Based Image Production, Jg. 19 (2023), Nr. 1, S. 121–134. DOI: https://doi.org/10.25969/mediarep/22316.

Olayode, I. O., Du, B., Severino, A., Campisi, T., & Alex, F. J. (2023). Systematic literature review on the applications, impacts, and public perceptions of autonomous vehicles in road transportation system. *Journal of Traffic and Transportation Engineering (English edition)*, 10(6), 1037–1060, ISSN 2095–7564, https://doi.org/10.1016/j.jtte.2023.07.006.

Özalp, R., Varol, N. K., Taşci, B., & Uçar, A. (2020). A review of deep reinforcement learning algorithms and comparative results on inverted pendulum system. In *Machine learning paradigms: Advances in deep learning-based technological applications* (pp. 237–256). Springer.

Persico, V., Montieri, A., & Pescape, A. (2016, October). On the network performance of amazon S3 cloud-storage service. In *2016 5th IEEE international conference on cloud networking (Cloudnet)* (pp. 113–118). IEEE.

Peterson, L. E. (2009). K-nearest neighbor. *Scholarpedia*, 4(2), 1883.

Pietrzak, M., & Baran, J. (2007). *Podstawy zarządzania. Studia przypadków i inne ćwiczenia aktywizujące*. Warszawa: SGGW.

Polato, I., Ré, R., Goldman, A., & Kon, F. (2014). A comprehensive view of Hadoop research – A systematic literature review. *Journal of Network and Computer Applications*, 46, 1–25.

Prakash, S., & Verma, A. K. (2022). Anthropogenic activities and biodiversity threats. *International Journal of Biological Innovations*, 4(1), 94–103.

Przegalińska, A., Będkowski, M., Brdulak, J., Fazlagić, J., Janiszewski, M., Jemielniak, D., Kornowska, L., Piekarski, C., Rabiega-Wiśniewska, J., Stęchły, J., Stęchły, W., Szołtysek, J., Sysło, M., M., & Usidus, M. (2022). *Sztuczna inteligencja (AI) jako megatrend kształtujący edukację Jak przygotowywać się na szanse i wyzwania społeczno-gospodarcze związane ze sztuczną inteligencją?* Warszawa: Instytut Badań Edukacyjnych

Qian, J., Song, Z., Yao, Y., Zhu, Z., & Zhang, X. (2022). A review on autoencoder based representation learning for fault detection and diagnosis in industrial processes. *Chemometrics and Intelligent Laboratory Systems*, 231, 104711.

Qian, L., Luo, Z., Du, Y., & Guo, L. (2009). Cloud computing: An overview. In *Cloud computing: First international conference, CloudCom 2009, Beijing, China, December 1–4, 2009. Proceedings 1* (pp. 626–631). Springer Berlin Heidelberg.

Ragin, Ch., & Becker, H. (1992). *What is a case? Exploring the foundations of social inquiry*. Cambridge: Cambridge University Press.

Rajpurohit, A. M., Kumar, P., Kumar, R. R., & Kumar, R. (2023). A review on Apache Spark. *Kilby*, 100, 7.

Rana, M. S., Nobi, M. N., Murali, B., & Sung, A. H. (2022). Deepfake detection: A systematic literature review. *IEEE Access*, 10, 25494–25513.

Rani, V., Nabi, S. T., Kumar, M., Mittal, A., & Kumar, K. (2023). Self-supervised learning: A succinct review. *Archives of Computational Methods in Engineering*, 30(4), 2761–2775.

Raptis, T. P., & Passarella, A. (2023). A survey on networked data streaming with apache kafka. *IEEE access*, 11, 85333–85350.

Regenwetter, L., Nobari, A. H., & Ahmed, F. (2022). Deep generative models in engineering design: A review. *Journal of Mechanical Design*, 144(7), 071704.

Reinhardt, K. (2023). Trust and trustworthiness in AI ethics. *AI and Ethics*, 3(3), 735–744.

Report of the World Commission on Environment and Development. (1987). *Our common future*. Oslo: United Nations.

Rezaei, F., Safavi, H. R., Abd Elaziz, M., & Mirjalili, S. (2023). GMO: Geometric mean optimizer for solving engineering problems. *Soft Computing*, 27(15), 10571–10606.

Ronzhyn, A., Cardenal, A. S., & Batlle Rubio, A. (2023). Defining affordances in social media research: A literature review. *New Media & Society*, 25(11), 3165–3188.

Ryen, V., Soylu, A., & Roman, D. (2022). Building semantic knowledge graphs from (semi-) structured data: A review. *Future Internet*, 14(5), 129.

Sadee, W., Wang, D., Hartmann, K., & Toland, A. E. (2023). Pharmacogenomics: Driving personalized medicine. *Pharmacological Reviews*, 75(4), 789–814.

Safi, A., & Singh, S. (2023). A systematic literature review on phishing website detection techniques. *Journal of King Saud University-Computer and Information Sciences*, 35(2), 590–611.

Sagiroglu, S., & Sinanc, D. (2013, May). Big data: A review. In *2013 international conference on collaboration technologies and systems (CTS)* (pp. 42–47). IEEE.

Salloum, S., Dautov, R., Chen, X., Peng, P. X., & Huang, J. Z. (2016). Big data analytics on Apache Spark. *International Journal of Data Science and Analytics*, 1, 145–164.

Sánchez, J. (2014). Nuclear fusion as a massive, clean, and inexhaustible energy source for the second half of the century: Brief history, status, and perspective. *Energy Science & Engineering*, 2(4), 165–176.

Sanchez, S. A., Romero, H. J., & Morales, A. D. (2020, May). A review: Comparison of performance metrics of pretrained models for object detection using the TensorFlow framework. In *IOP conference series: Materials science and engineering* (Vol. 844, No. 1, p. 012024). IOP Publishing.

Santomartino, R., Averesch, N. J., Bhuiyan, M., Cockell, C. S., Colangelo, J., Gumulya, Y., . . . Zea, L. (2023). Toward sustainable space exploration: A roadmap for harnessing the power of microorganisms. *Nature Communications*, 14(1), 1391.

Santoso, M. H. (2021). Application of association rule method using apriori algorithm to find sales patterns case study of Indomaret Tanjung Anom. *Brilliance: Research of Artificial Intelligence*, 1(2), 54–66.

Saraswat, P., & Raj, S. (2021). A review paper on Hadoop architecture. *International Journal of Innovative Research in Computer Science & Technology*, 9(6), 96–99.

Setiyadi, A., & Setiawan, E. B. (2023, October). Comparative analysis of interactive map data loading using the GeoJSON method for West Java new entrepreneurs. In *2023 international conference on informatics engineering, science & technology (INCITEST)* (pp. 1–4). IEEE.

Shafi, M., Molisch, A. F., Smith, P. J., Haustein, T., Zhu, P., De Silva, P., . . . Wunder, G. (2017). 5G: A tutorial overview of standards, trials, challenges, deployment, and practice. *IEEE Journal on Selected Areas in Communications*, 35(6), 1201–1221.

Shafiullah, N. M. M., Rai, A., Etukuru, H., Liu, Y., Misra, I., Chintala, S., & Pinto, L. (2023). On bringing robots home. *arXiv preprint* arXiv:2311.16098.

Shapira, A., & Dvir, T. (2021). 3D tissue and organ printing – hope and reality. *Advanced Science*, 8(10), 2003751.

Sharma, D. K., Singh, N. C., Noola, D. A., Doss, A. N., & Sivakumar, J. (2022). A review on various cryptographic techniques & algorithms. *Materials Today: Proceedings*, 51, 104–109.

Sharma, K., Arora, A., & Tripathi, S. K. (2019). Review of supercapacitors: Materials and devices. *Journal of Energy Storage*, 21, 801–825.

Sharma, P., Dash, B., & Ansari, M. F. (2022). Anti-phishing techniques – a review of Cyber Defense Mechanisms. *International Journal of Advanced Research in Computer and Communication Engineering ISO*, 3297, 2007.

Sheikh, A. (2021). Trojans, backdoors, viruses, and worms. In *Certified Ethical Hacker (CEH) preparation guide: Lesson-based review of ethical hacking and penetration testing* (pp. 49–69). Berkeley, CA: Apress.

Sheykhmousa, M., Mahdianpari, M., Ghanbari, H., Mohammadimanesh, F., Ghamisi, P., & Homayouni, S. (2020). Support vector machine versus random forest for remote sensing image classification: A meta-analysis and systematic review. *IEEE Journal of Selected Topics in Applied Earth Observations and Remote Sensing*, 13, 6308–6325.

Shum, H. Y., He, X. D., & Li, D. (2018). From Eliza to XiaoIce: Challenges and opportunities with social chatbots. *Frontiers of Information Technology & Electronic Engineering*, 19, 10–26.

Sirota, S. (2021). Despite limitations, USAF operators seeking new missions for MQ-9 Reaper. *Inside the Air Force*, 32(9), 1–7.

Skolik, A., Jerbi, S., & Dunjko, V. (2022). Quantum agents in the gym: A variational quantum algorithm for deep q-learning. *Quantum*, 6, 720.

Skoumpakis, S. (2016). Eindhoven: Technische Universiteit Eindhoven. *Hue bridge-lighting automation engine: Investigate lighting control alternatives for the existing rule-engine*, p. 83.

Snehi, M., & Bhandari, A. (2021, March). Apprehending Mirai botnet philosophy and smart learning models for IoT-DDoS detection. In *2021 8th international conference on computing for sustainable global development (INDIACom)* (pp. 501–505). IEEE.

Solanki, V. K., & Dhall, R. (2017). An IoT based predictive connected car maintenance approach. *Int. J. Interact. Multim. Artif. Intell.* 4(2017), 16–22.

Strelkova, O., & Pasichnyk, O. (2017). *Three Types of Artificial Intelligence*, http://eztuir.ztu.edu.ua/bitstream/handle/123456789/6479/142.pdf?sequence=1&i (access: 19.01.2026).

Su, X., Yan, X., & Tsai, C. L. (2012). Linear regression. *Wiley Interdisciplinary Reviews: Computational Statistics*, 4(3), 275–294.

Suarez-Tangil, G., Tapiador, J. E., Peris-Lopez, P., & Ribagorda, A. (2013). Evolution, detection and analysis of malware for smart devices. *IEEE Communications Surveys & Tutorials*, 16(2), 961–987.

Szeliski, R. (2022). *Computer vision: Algorithms and applications*. Springer Nature.

Świechowski, M., Godlewski, K., Sawicki, B., & Mańdziuk, J. (2023). Monte Carlo tree search: A review of recent modifications and applications. *Artificial Intelligence Review*, 56(3), 2497–2562.

Tang, C., Wang, Y., Li, Y., Zeng, S., Kong, L., Li, L., . . . Deng, T. (2023). A review of graphene-based temperature sensors. *Microelectronic Engineering*, 278, 112015.

Tatam, M., Shanmugam, B., Azam, S., & Kannoorpatti, K. (2021). A review of threat modelling approaches for APT-style attacks. *Heliyon*, 7(1).

Thacker, U., Pandey, M., & Rautaray, S. S. (2018). Review of Elasticsearch Performance Variating the Indexing Methods. In *Progress in intelligent computing techniques: Theory, practice, and applications: Proceedings of ICACNI 2016* (Vol. 2, pp. 3–8). Springer Singapore.

Thomas, T. W., Tabassum, M., Chu, B., & Lipford, H. (2018, April). Security during application development: An application security expert perspective. In *Proceedings of the 2018 CHI conference on human factors in computing systems* (pp. 1–12). Association for Computing Machinery.

Tong, Y., Liu, H., & Zhang, Z. (2024). Advancements in humanoid robots: A comprehensive review and future prospects. *IEEE/CAA Journal of Automatica Sinica*, 11(2), 301–328.

Torromé, R. G., & Barzanjeh, S. (2024). Advances in quantum radar and quantum LiDAR. *Progress in Quantum Electronics*, 93, 100497.

Tulshan, A. S., & Dhage, S. N. (2019). Survey on virtual assistant: Google Assistant, Siri, Cortana, Alexa. In *Advances in signal processing and intelligent recognition systems: 4th international symposium SIRS 2018, Bangalore, India, September 19–22, 2018, revised selected papers 4* (pp. 190–201). Springer Singapore.

Ugwuishiwu, C. H., Orji, U. E., Ugwu, C. I., & Asogwa, C. N. (2020). An overview of quantum cryptography and Shor's algorithm. *International Journal of Advanced Trends in Computer Science and Engineering*, 9(5).

Van de Sande, D., Van Genderen, M. E., Smit, J. M., Huiskens, J., Visser, J. J., Veen, R. E., . . . van Bommel, J. (2022). Developing, implementing and governing artificial intelligence in medicine: A step-by-step approach to prevent an artificial intelligence winter. *BMJ Health & Care Informatics*, 29(1).

Viloria, A., Acuña, G. C., Franco, D. J. A., Hernández-Palma, H., Fuentes, J. P., & Rambal, E. P. (2019). Integration of data mining techniques to PostgreSQL database manager system. *Procedia Computer Science*, 155, 575–580.

Walancik, M. (2007). *Zmiana społeczna a opinie poborowych o zasadniczej służbie wojskowej*. Kraków: Oficyna Wydawnicza "Impuls".

Walancik, M. (2015). Wybrane współczesne zagrożenia niemilitarne. Traby powietrzne, szadź na ternie województwa śląskiego. [In:] P. Polko & M. Walancik (red.), *Praktyczne aspekty współdziałania Trenowych Organów Administracji Wojskowej i administracji publicznej w sytuacjach kryzysowych*. Dąbrowa Górnicza: Wydawnictwo Naukowe Wyższej Szkoły Biznesu w Dąbrowie Górniczej.

Wang, J., Shao, Y., Ge, Y., & Yu, R. (2019). A survey of vehicle to everything (V2X) testing. *Sensors*, 19(2), 334.

Weiser, M. (1999). The computer for the 21st century. *ACM SIGMOBILE Mobile Computing and Communications Review*, 3(3), 3–11.

Wu, T., He, S., Liu, J., Sun, S., Liu, K., Han, Q. L., & Tang, Y. (2023). A brief overview of ChatGPT: The history, status quo and potential future development. *IEEE/CAA Journal of Automatica Sinica*, 10(5), 1122–1136.

Xu, Y. (2016). A general comparison between tokamak and stellarator plasmas. *Matter and Radiation at Extremes*, 1(4), 192–200.

Xue, Y. (2019). A review on intelligent wearables: Uses and risks. *Human Behavior and Emerging Technologies*, 1(4), 287–294.

Yanamala, A. K. Y., & Suryadevara, S. (2024). Navigating data protection challenges in the era of artificial intelligence: A comprehensive review. *Revista de Inteligencia Artificial en Medicina*, 15(1), 113–146.

Yenduri, G., Ramalingam, M., Selvi, G. C., Supriya, Y., Srivastava, G., Maddikunta, P. K. R., . . . Gadekallu, T. R. (2024). GPT (Generative Pre-trained Transformer)–A comprehensive review on enabling technologies, potential applications, emerging challenges, and future directions. *Journal of Intelligent Learning Systems and Applications*, 16(4), IEEE Access.

Younan, M., Houssein, E. H., Elhoseny, M., & Ali, A. A. (2020). Challenges and recommended technologies for the industrial internet of things: A comprehensive review. *Measurement*, 151, 107198.

Yu, D. G., Li, Q., Song, W., Xu, L., Zhang, K., & Zhou, T. (2023). Advanced technique-based combination of innovation education and safety education in higher education. *Journal of Chemical Education*, 100(2), 507–516.

Zalewska-Bochenko, A. (2024). Sztuczna inteligencja w procesie edukacji. *Optimum Economic Studies*, 116(2), 194–210.

Zhang, J., Koppel, A., Bedi, A. S., Szepesvari, C., & Wang, M. (2020). Variational policy gradient method for reinforcement learning with general utilities. *Advances in Neural Information Processing Systems*, 33, 4572–4583.

Zhou, C., Li, Q., Li, C., Yu, J., Liu, Y., Wang, G., . . . Sun, L. (2023). A comprehensive survey on pretrained foundation models: A history from Bert to ChatGPT. *arXiv preprint* arXiv:2302.09419.

Zhu, K., & Zhang, T. (2021). Deep reinforcement learning based mobile robot navigation: A review. *Tsinghua Science and Technology*, 26(5), 674–691.

Żyliński, A., Klonowska, I., Bekulard, B., & Kobuszewski, M. (red.). (2024). *Nowe zjawiska w dobie pandemii Covid-19. Perspektywa kryminalna i kryminologiczna*. Szczytno.

Гойденко, В. К., & Рожнов, А. В. (2022). О ПРЕЦЕДЕНТЕ ПРИМЕНЕНИЯ АВТОНОМНОГО РЕЖИМА НАВЕДЕНИЯ БЕСПИЛОТНОЙ АВИАЦИО ННОЙ СИСТЕМЫ “STM КАРГУ-2”.

Online sources

Convention. (1972). https://web.archive.org/web/20101229234941/www.opbw.org/convention/conv.html, accessed 21 January 2025.

Data. (2020). www.storagenewsletter.com/2021/03/25/64-2zb-of-data-created-or-replicated-in-2020, accessed 13 December 2024.

Katastrofa. (1990). *Mining disaster at the Halemba mine*. https://pl.wikipedia.org/wiki/Katastrofa_g%C3%B3rnicza_w_kopalni_Halemba_(1990), accessed 3 March 2025.

Katastrofa. (2006). *Mining disaster at the Halemba mine*. https://pl.wikipedia.org/wiki/Katastrofa_g%C3%B3rnicza_w_kopalni_Halemba_(2006), accessed 3 March 2025.

Katastrofa. (2022). *Mining disaster at the Borynia-Zofiówka mine*. https://pl.wikipedia.org/wiki/Katastrofa_g%C3%B3rnicza_w_kopalni_Zofi%C3%B3wka_(2022), accessed 3 March 2025.

Kolej. (2019). *Metropolitan railway*. https://metropoliagzm.pl/kolej-metropolitalna, accessed 4 March 2025.

Mobilność. (2019). *Sustainable mobility.* https://metropoliagzm.pl/zrownowazona-mobilnosc/, accessed 4 March 2025.

Raport. (2021). *Annual report JSW.* www.jsw.pl/raportroczny-2021/zrownowazony-rozwoj-w-jsw/dbalosc-o-bezpieczenstwo, accessed 4 March 2025.

RODO. (2016). Regulation (EU) 2016/679 of the European Parliament and of the Council of 27 April 2016 on the protection of natural persons with regard to the processing of personal data and on the free movement of such data and repealing Directive 95/46/EC (General Data Protection Regulation). https://uodo.gov.pl/pl/131/224, accessed 20 January 2025.

Strategia. (2023). *Development strategy for the upper Silesian Metropolis 2022–2027, with an outlook to 2035 executive summary.* https://infogzm.metropoliagzm.pl/wp-content/uploads/2023/07/streszczenie-website_pl.pdf, accessed 3 March 2025.

Szczeliny. (2022). *Cracks in Jaworzno.* https://dziennikzachodni.pl/w-jaworznie-zapadla-sie-ziemia-szczelina-siega-10-metrow-sluzby-pracuja-na-miejscu-droga-zamknieta/ar/c1–16917605, accessed 3 March 2025.

UstawaKSB. (2018). https://isap.sejm.gov.pl/isap.nsf/download.xsp/WDU20180001560/U/D20181560Lj.pdf, accessed 20 January 2025.

Wypadki. (2022). *Accidents in the mining industry.* www.slaskibiznes.pl/wiadomosci,w-2022-roku-wiecej-wypadkow-w-kopalniach-wyzszy-urzad-gorniczy-przed stawia-liczby,wia5-1-7961.html, accessed 3 March 2025.

WypadkiWUG. (2022). *Accidents by WUG.* www.wug.gov.pl/o_nas/wiadomosci_wug/Stan-bezpieczenstwa-pracy-w-gornictwie-w-2022-r/idn:3937, accessed 3 March 2025.

Wypadkowość. (2022). *Accident rates in mining.* www.wug.gov.pl/o_nas/wiadomosci_wug/Stan-bezpieczenstwa-pracy-w-gornictwie-w-2022-r/idn:3937, accessed 4 March 2025.

Index